365 MEDITATIONS FOR TEENS

Sally D. Sharpe, Editor

Steve Broderson, Ken and Liz Carter,
Thomas Charlton, Christopher Cropsey,
Harriette Cross, Clare Golson Doyle,
Anne Marie Drew, Tai Gregory, Reginia Guess,
Kwasi Kena, Al and Sharon Meeds,
John William Peterson, Helen J. Stanphill,
Matthew D. Stultz

Dimensions for Living
Nashville

This book is printed on recycled, acid-free paper.

Library of Congress Cataloging-in-Publication Data

365 Meditations for teens / Sally D. Sharpe, editor ; Steve Broderson ... [et al.].
  p. cm.
  ISBN 0-687-08807-0
  1. Teenagers—Prayer-books and devotions—English. 2. Devotional calendars—Methodist Church.   I. Title: Three hundred sixty-five meditations for teens. II. Sharpe, Sally D., 1964- III. Broderson, Steve.

BV4850 .A14 2000
242'.63—dc21

00-031440

00 01 02 03 04 05 06 07 08 09—10 9 8 7 6 5 4 3 2 1

MANUFACTURED IN THE UNITED STATES OF AMERICA

CONTENTS

INTRODUCTION

We live in a rapidly changing world. At times things seem to be changing faster than we can keep up. The newest advances in technology are obsolete within one to three years. Even the latest trends in fashion and music seem to have shorter "life spans" these days. But despite all the changes taking place around us, there are some things that haven't changed—such as what it's like to be a teenager.

"Wait a minute," you say. "My parents had it much easier than I do. It's nothing like it was in their day." There's no doubt that times have changed. And few would disagree that we seem to live in a more dangerous, volatile world today. Yet regardless of how times change, many of the basic emotions, struggles, victories, fears, joys, and questions that accompany the teen years remain the same from generation to generation.

What do other people think of me?
Will I be successful at what I do—now and in the future?
What if I "goof up"—or fail?
What's going to happen to me—next week, next month, next year, the rest of my life?
When did my parents stop being as smart as they used to be?
Will they ever understand me?
When will I meet "the one" for me, and how will I know?
Is there a God, and does God really care about me?

The list of questions and uncertainties goes on and on. You could add twenty more to the list without blinking; so could anyone who has "been there." Believe it or not, the adults you think don't have a clue about how you feel actually know more than you give them credit for. Maybe they haven't had exactly the same experiences you've had, but they've had many similar ones. They made it through the tumultuous teen years, and they learned a little something along the way. They'd love to share it with you, no doubt, if they had the opportunity. But those opportunities are few and far between; and besides, it can be awkward and embarrassing to open up and *really talk* with some adults, right?

That's why this book is so great—it gives you the opportunity to anonymously "listen in" as twelve adults share insights and words of wisdom about life and faith and many of the specific questions and concerns that are so important to you right now. They write as men, women, mothers, fathers, youth leaders, pastors, counselors, teachers, students, business professionals, musicians, and, most of all, as Christians who care deeply about young people just like you. Though each writer has his or her own personality and style, you will find a common theme among them: encouragement. They want you to know that although the teen years bring great growing pains, they also bring great joys and celebrations. They want you to know that although you sometimes feel rejected, alone, or afraid, God loves you unconditionally and is always there for you. They want you to know that although the world around you is constantly changing, God is unchanging; and if you put your faith in the never-failing love of God, you will find yourself standing on a foundation that cannot be shaken when the things of this world seem to be tumbling down around you—or even down upon you!

I invite you to take a journey with these writers over the next twelve months, stopping along the way to consider not only what it means to have faith, but also what it looks like to live out that faith every day of your life. You'll especially enjoy the month of July, when you take a "detour" with four of your peers who share their own faith as they explore important issues from a teen's perspective. There's no preparation for this trip, and it won't take up much of your time—just a couple of minutes each day. So get ready for an incredible adventure. Your guaranteed destination is a closer relationship with God.

Sally D. Sharpe, Editor

ABOUT THE WRITERS

STEVE BRODERSON (MARCH) is the chaplain and communications coordinator for the Kentucky United Methodist Homes for Children and Youth. Previously he has worked as an on-air personality for a Christian radio station, an interim youth minister, and a graphic designer. He enjoys writing and recording music in a home studio and occasionally produces independent Christian artists. Steve has written for *Reel to Real Magazine* and *Nautilus CD Magazine*. He and his wife, Julie, live in Versailles, Kentucky.

KEN CARTER (FEBRUARY) and **LIZ CARTER** (FEBRUARY / JULY) are a father-daughter duo who have collaborated on several projects together. Ken is senior pastor of Mount Tabor United Methodist Church in Winston-Salem, North Carolina. His writings have appeared in *Christian Century, Upper Room, Alive Now,* and the *Journal of Pastoral Care.* His hobbies are tennis, travel, and music. Liz, who also is one of the teen contributors for the month of July, is a ninth grader whose hobbies include reading (fantasy and science fiction), listening to music—especially the Beatles—and visiting chat rooms on the Web. With her dad, she has written curriculum for youth based on the movie *X-Files: Fight the Future,* appearing in the publication *Reel to Real,* and currently she is working on a book of poems.

THOMAS CHARLTON (JULY) is a nineteen-year-old student from Gallatin, Tennessee. He attends the University of Tennessee, Knoxville.

CHRISTOPHER CROPSEY (JULY) is an eighteen-year-old student from Mt. Juliet, Tennessee. He is a freshman piano performance major and honor student at Belmont University in Nashville, Tennessee, and is active in Bible study at school and at Grace United Methodist Church. He enjoys music and running track and cross country.

HARRIETTE CROSS (MAY) lives in Aurora, Illinois, with her twelve-year-old son, Prentice. She is Associate Pastor at Wesley United Methodist church where she works primarily with the children and youth. Her greatest joy is seeing a young person grow in faith in Christ.

CLARE GOLSON DOYLE (AUGUST) is a full-time mother of two children: Elizabeth, age seven, and Allen, age four. She holds a Masters of Divinity from Vanderbilt University and has worked in higher education, camping ministry, and pastoral care. Clare has been working with youth for over eighteen years in the North Alabama, Memphis, and Tennessee Annual Conferences of The United Methodist Church. She is very active in Christian education, leading workshops, teaching Sunday school classes, and planning programs. She lives with her family in Waverly, Tennessee, where her husband, Lloyd, is a United Methodist pastor.

ANNE MARIE DREW (APRIL) teaches at the United States Naval Academy in Annapolis, Maryland, where she is the director of Masqueraders, a student theater group. She is the author of several books, including *Empty Nest, Full Life, The Innkeeper's Wife: And Four Other Dramatic Readings for Christmas,* and *Rainbows in the Twelfth Row,* a novel for young readers. She also has contributed to *365 Meditations for Teachers.* She has three grown children.

TAI GREGORY (JULY) is a fifteen-year-old sophomore at McGavock High School in Nashville, Tennessee, where she is treasurer of FCA and is involved in the band program, cheerleading, and softball. She attends Hermitage United Methodist Church and is active in the youth program, drama group, youth choir, and youth council. Tai says that the biggest part of her life always has and always will be God. She believes that if you have the kind of faith that moves mountains and love for God in your heart, you will always end up "at the top."

REGINIA GUESS (SEPTEMBER) is a student assistance specialist at Franklin High School in Franklin, Tennessee. She also has worked as an alcohol and drug treatment counselor with adults, teens, and children. She has enjoyed writing since she was a child, writing mostly poems, short stories, and articles for various newspapers and newsletters. Reginia and her eleven-year-old daughter make their home in Nashville, Tennessee.

KWASI KENA (JUNE) has taught numerous collegiate courses in communication, social science, and religion, and has written curriculum and devotional materials for Urban Ministries, Cokesbury, and Abingdon Press. His latest publication is *Forty Days in the Wilderness,* a devotional book for African American men. Kwasi and his wife, Safiyah Fosua, have two sons, Tony and Chris. Kwasi and Safiyah are currently serving their second three-year term as missionaries to Ghana, West Africa. Formerly, they were jointly appointed as pastors to the Jubilee United Methodist Church in Waterloo, Iowa. Kwasi's hobbies include reading, listening to music from around the world, studying foreign languages, designing clothing, and sketching.

AL AND SHARON MEEDS (DECEMBER) share the duties of Youth Director at Renton First United Methodist Church in

Renton, Washington. Sharon also works part time as the Camping and Convo registrar for the Pacific Northwest Annual Conference of The United Methodist Church. Previously she has held jobs as a chef, choir director, and a computer operator. Al has worked for State Farm Insurance for over twenty years and currently serves as a specialist on large scale building damages and as a fire investigator. He has worked previously as a farm worker, lumberjack, and carpenter. Both have been involved in music much of their lives, participating in vocal choirs, handbell choirs, and currently the Good Medicine Music Ministry.

JOHN WILLIAM PETERSON (OCTOBER) is an ordained United Methodist minister and a freelance writer. He writes regularly for Cokesbury curriculum resources *LinC* (Living in Christ) and *Faithlink*. John also enjoys reading and bicycling. He lives in Gig Harbor, Washington.

HELEN J. STANPHILL (JANUARY) has worked extensively with youth in grades 6-12 for the past seven years in both the United States and England. She has a passion for helping youth recognize and contrast the themes found in TV shows, movies, magazines, and music with the truth found in God's Word. Currently she ministers to middle school and senior high students at Community Bible Church in San Antonio, Texas.

MATTHEW D. STULTZ (NOVEMBER) is a seminary student pursuing two master's degrees at Methodist Theological School in Ohio, and is currently serving as a student pastor to Fowlerton United Methodist Church in Fowlerton, Indiana. In addition to earning three undergraduate degrees, he has studied in England, done missions work in Jamaica, and performed in numerous musicals, plays, and ensembles. Matthew and his wife, Heather, are the proud "parents" of an eighty-pound yellow Labrador named Hercules.

JANUARY

POPULAR CULTURE: COMPARING GOD'S VALUES TO THE WORLD'S VALUES

Helen J. Stanphill

POPULAR CULTURE: COMPARING GOD'S VALUES TO THE WORLD'S VALUES

Helen J. Stanphill

JANUARY 1 — GOD'S VALUES

Whatever is true, whatever is noble, whatever is right, whatever is pure, whatever is lovely, whatever is admirable—if anything is excellent or praiseworthy—think about such things. Whatever you have learned or received or heard from me, or seen in me—put it into practice. And the God of peace will be with you.

—Philippians 4:8-9

Generally speaking, the secular world's values are practically the opposites of the ones that Paul describes here. So, as Christians, we constantly need to refer to Scripture to keep ourselves focused on God's values. This month we will look at how the values reflected in popular culture compare to God's values, which we find in the Bible. We'll look at a lot of different things, from video games and movies to music and the World Wide Web. You'll have a chance to think about how you spend your free time and how you can honor God with every area of your life. We'll look at what God wants us to fill our minds and hearts with, and why.

For starters, list the qualities that are pleasing to God from the passage above. Next to each quality, write an example of someone or something that fits the description—either from the Bible or from your own life.

God, when I am confronted today with anything that conflicts with your values, turn my mind to the true, noble, right, and praiseworthy things that I see in your Word and in the life of Jesus. Amen.

JANUARY 2 — THE SIN TRAP

We know that the law is spiritual; but I am unspiritual, sold as a slave to sin. I do not understand what I do. For what I want to do I do not do, but what I hate I do. . . For I have the desire to do

what is good, but I cannot carry it out. For what I do is not the good I want to do;
no, the evil I do not want to do—this I keep on doing. —Romans 7:14-15, 18b-19

Have you ever noticed that it is usually much easier to do the wrong thing than to do the right thing? For instance, cheating on a test is easier than studying and learning the material yourself. Getting drunk is easier than standing up to peer pressing or dealing with the problems you may be trying to escape from by using alcohol. Paul knew all about this tendency to sin, because he himself wanted to do right but found that he did not have the strength to carry it out. Before we can go any further in understanding God's values, we have to understand Paul's point in this passage: We constantly struggle with sin, and the ability to triumph over sin does not come from our own strength.

In the past week, how have you caved in to sin? Why do you think you did so?

Lord, help me see the sin in my life clearly, and give me the desire to honor you by doing the right thing in all areas of my life. Amen.

 # NO CONDEMNATION

Therefore, there is now no condemnation for those who are in Christ Jesus, because through Christ Jesus the law of the Spirit of life set me free from the law of sin and death.
—Romans 8:1-2

Yes, sin is a constant struggle, but the GREAT news is that Jesus has won the sin battle for us! He lived a sinless life and gave his life on the cross, taking the punishment we deserved for our sins. Our sin separates us from God, who is holy and perfect. But Jesus laid down his life as a bridge between us and God, so that we could cross over from the condemnation that follows sin to the promise of eternal life with God. Jesus offers this free gift to all who ask. Though we still will struggle with sin in this broken world, as followers of Christ, we are no longer destined for eternal punishment because of our sin. The Holy Spirit works within our hearts to give us the desire to honor the Lord in all things. But first, we have to accept God's free gift of forgiveness and salvation! To do so, say this prayer:

Lord, I've made a lot of mistakes. Forgive me for all that I've done wrong and for how I've turned away from you. Thank you for providing Jesus to take the punishment I deserve by dying on the cross. Please come and live within my heart. Take charge of my life so that it brings you honor. I'm ready to live for you. Amen.

JANUARY 4 — RENEWED MINDS, TRANSFORMED LIVES

Therefore, I urge you. . . . in view of God's mercy, to offer your bodies as living sacrifices, holy and pleasing to God—this is your spiritual act of worship. Do not conform any longer to the pattern of this world, but be transformed by the renewing of your mind. Then you will be able to test and approve what God's will is—his good, pleasing and perfect will. —Romans 12:1-2

Have you ever felt squeezed into a mold that doesn't fit you? Maybe the "in crowd" at school has done that to you, or perhaps your friends have pressured you to do something that you know is at odds with God's desires for your life.

How *does* God want us to live? This passage tells us that in light of all the love and mercy the Lord has so generously given us, we are to give our lives completely to him. We are to live in a way that is pure, right, and pleasing to him. Wow! That sounds impossible! Well, it is—without the work of the Holy Spirit in us to renew our minds and transform our lives.

Think of two of your attitudes or values that belong more to the world than to God. Ask him now to begin showing you his point of view on those issues.

Lord, when I chase after things that do not honor you, reveal to me the emptiness and the self-centered nature of this world. May your Spirit change my heart and renew my mind, filling me with a desire to love, honor, and serve you in everything that I am and everything that I do. Amen.

JANUARY 5 — THE BELIEVER'S FREEDOM

"Everything is permissible"—but not everything is beneficial. "Everything is permissible"—but not everything is constructive. Nobody should seek his own good, but the good of others. . . . So whether you eat or drink or whatever you do, do it all for the glory of God. —1 Corinthians 10:23-24, 31

Paul probably is quoting a saying that was popular in the young Corinthian church, an attitude of "I can do anything because God's grace and forgiveness have saved me." This attitude can cause problems if something a Christian does causes another believer to stumble in his or her faith. In this case, the issue was whether Christians could eat meat sacrificed to idols. Some said it was OK, because they knew the idols were worthless compared to Christ. For other believers, eating that meat would cause them to go back to their old ways of worshiping idols, so they needed to avoid that practice completely.

What three main guidelines does Paul give here for deciding whether something you like to do honors God? To glorify God is to put the focus on God—rather than on yourself—and make God look good to others. Is there anything you do that might cause some believers to stumble?

> Holy Spirit, please show me when I do anything that is not beneficial or constructive to me or to other people. Give me a sensitive heart, so that I am not just concerned about my own freedom. Instead, make me truly interested in the good of others, especially when I can help encourage their faith. Amen.

JANUARY 6 POWER OF THE WORD

In the beginning was the Word, and the Word was with God, and the Word was God. He was with God in the beginning. . . . In him was life, and that life was the light of men. —John 1:1-2, 4

Words are such powerful things. By God's word, the heavens and the earth were created (see Genesis 1). In this passage from John, the author goes back to the time before Creation to explain that the Word was with God from the beginning of all things. We understand from verse 4 that this Word was Jesus Christ. After Creation, God spoke to humankind by giving Moses the law and by communicating through the prophets' teachings to repent of sin and worship the one true God. Still, many ignored these words from God. So God sent his Son, Jesus, to give us the "last word" on salvation and on loving God. We have complete access to all these words of God in the Bible. Of all the things at God's disposal to teach us and lead us, God has relied most on the Word spoken, written, and incarnated in Christ.

> Almighty Creator and author of life, help me understand the awesome power of language. Use the words I speak to glorify your name, to build up those around me, and to work for all kinds of good in this world. Amen.

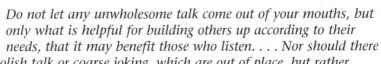

JANUARY 7 — TAMING THE TONGUE

Do not let any unwholesome talk come out of your mouths, but only what is helpful for building others up according to their needs, that it may benefit those who listen. . . . Nor should there be obscenity, foolish talk or coarse joking, which are out of place, but rather thanksgiving. —Ephesians 4:29, 5:4

How does the advice in these verses compare with the last comedian you heard or the usual dialogue in your favorite TV show? How do your conversations with friends stack up against this measure? The Bible is full of warnings about the power of the spoken word to hurt others or to damage your witness as a Christian. The basic theme is this: What comes out of your mouth is a reflection of what's in your heart.

Look for ways to encourage others through your conversation. Take a challenge from Paul in these verses and listen to yourself for a day. How much of what you say benefits those who listen, and how much is just foolish talk or gossip? How often do obscenities and profanity pop into your head and/or out of your mouth? Ask God to help you speak with wisdom and grace, as Christ did.

God, I want to bring you honor and to encourage others with my words. Change my heart so that the coarse talk and obscenity that offend you also offend me. Teach me to choose my words wisely and to think about the impact my words will have before I speak. Amen.

JANUARY 8 — HONORING GOD'S NAME

But I tell you, Do not swear at all: either by heaven, for it is God's throne; or by the earth, for it is his footstool; or by Jerusalem, for it is the city of the Great King . . . Simply let your "Yes" be "Yes," and your "No," "No"; anything beyond this comes from the evil one. —Matthew 5:34-35, 37

Making solemn vows or oaths before God was a common practice in Old Testament times; but in Jesus' time, it appears that many people were making promises to God using big words without really intending to keep the vow. Or worse yet, they were using God's name for trivial or sinful stuff. This sounds a lot like us today, when we say things like, "I swear to God, if you don't shut up, I'll . . ." or, "Oh, my God." Jesus tells us to give up this kind of swearing. All we need to say is yes or no—whether we are very serious, angry, or happy. Our word is enough. This admonition follows the solemn third commandment not to misuse God's name (see Exodus 20:7).

Today, count how many times you want to swear or actually do swear, and how many times you hear others swear (in real life, on TV, etc.).

Lord Jesus, there are so many times I let you down in this area. Give me the desire to honor you despite the many ways I hear your holy name abused every day. When I'm angry, help me work through it without taking your name in vain or using other language that dishonors you. Amen.

 # GOSSIP WOUNDS

Whoever belittles another lacks sense, but an intelligent person remains silent. A gossip goes about telling secrets, but one who is trustworthy in spirit keeps a confidence.
—*Proverbs 11:12-13 (NRSV)*

When was the last time you made fun of someone or cut someone down in front of his or her friends? Why did you do it? How does it feel when a friend betrays your trust?

Try to think of one character on your favorite TV show who sets a good example of keeping confidences and not gossiping. By contrast, how many shows can you name that revolve around gossip, deception, and betrayal? Some talk shows, daytime soap operas, and weeknight melodramas should come to mind. It is easy to say that these shows aren't real and therefore shouldn't matter; but be aware that by watching them, you are filling your mind with examples of behavior that do not honor Christ.

Loving Father, teach me how to truly love my neighbors so that I want what is best for them. Give me the words for helpful suggestions that are constructive, rather than cold-hearted criticism that is meant to belittle others or to make me feel superior to them. When I am tempted to gossip, remind me of how betrayal hurts others. Amen.

 # PSYCHIC STUFF

When [people] tell you to consult mediums and spiritists, who whisper and mutter, should not a people inquire of their God? Why consult the dead on behalf of the living? To the law and to the testimony! If they do not speak according to this word, they have no light of dawn.
—*Isaiah 8:19-20*

We are a society obsessed with knowing the future. From the psychic call-in lines advertised on TV to the horoscopes in daily newspapers, people are searching for answers and guidance. This passage shows us that the desire to foretell our future is nothing new. Guess what? God knows what's in our future and will guide us in all the decisions and choices that will get us there! Where do we look for this guidance?

Isaiah urges us to talk to and listen to God. He points us to God's law and the Bible's testimony about God in order to learn how God wants us to live and to make important decisions. Anything that does not ring true according to the Bible's teaching is worth nothing. The best news is that we don't have to worry or know everything that lies ahead because God is in control of everything.

> **Lord, sometimes I really want to know what lies ahead, and often I don't know what I should do when I'm faced with a tough decision. Draw me into prayer and into your Word so that I can learn how you want me to live. Reassure me that you are in control of everything and that you have a plan for my life. Amen.**

 # DO NOT WORRY

Therefore I tell you, do not worry about your life, what you will eat or drink; or about your body, what you will wear. Is not life more important than food, and the body more important than clothes? . . . For the pagans run after all these things, and your heavenly Father knows that you need them. But seek first his kingdom and his righteousness, and all these things will be given to you as well. —Matthew 6:25, 32-33

Why do you shop where you shop? How much does what you see everyone wearing at the mall influence what you buy? When it comes to your future, will you choose a career based on how much money you can earn? Or, are you looking for a career that will allow you to use your gifts in a way that keeps you focused on God?

The Father knows what we want, but he is primarily concerned with giving us what we really need—and he knows everything we need. If you're caught up with material stuff, take a moment to think about what's really important. If you often worry about your future, be assured that God is in control. Let his peace fill your heart as you pursue your goals, focused on honoring him in all that you do.

> **Heavenly Father, when I chase after the things of this world, remind me to seek first your kingdom and your righteousness. Replace my worries with confidence and trust in you. Amen.**

NEVER ENOUGH

Whoever loves money never has money enough; whoever loves wealth is never satisfied with his [or her] income. This too is meaningless. —Ecclesiastes 5:10

Have you ever noticed that the more money you have, the more you want? As the writer of Ecclesiastes was trying to make sense of life, he observed how meaningless and consuming the pursuit of wealth can be. In verse 15 of the same chapter, he notes that just as we come into this world with nothing, so also we will leave it with nothing.

What kind of commercials attract your attention most easily—those for cars, concerts, movies, clothes? The love of money and material possessions can easily become an idol that distracts you from God. Before you know it, you're a lot more concerned about how much stuff you have than about how much you love God. Learn to manage money wisely and enjoy it without setting your heart on material possessions. God wants your relationship with him and with the people you love to be your top priorities.

Lord, help me to find satisfaction in the work I do and to enjoy the money I earn without setting my heart on the things that money can buy. Help me to confront my own greed and turn my heart back toward you. Show me how to make my relationship with Jesus my greatest treasure in life. Amen.

ENVY

You shall not covet your neighbor's house. You shall not covet your neighbor's wife, or his manservant or maidservant, his ox or donkey, or anything that belongs to your neighbor.
—Exodus 20:17

Why do we want what other people have? Maybe we just want the stuff—clothes, car, stereo. Or, maybe we want the relationships others have—boyfriend/girlfriend, other friends, a less strict parent. Or, maybe we feel we're missing something—good looks, intelligence, personality, popularity. Coveting other people's stuff reveals that we doubt God's plan and provision for our lives.

Here's the antidote to envy. First, remember that God knows what you need and will meet your needs. God provides physical necessities as well as love, security, and purpose in life. Second, recognize that God wants to use you in big ways to build the Kingdom, but God doesn't measure success in the world's terms (money, prestige, power). God has created you with special gifts to fulfill his purposes for your life, and his plan for success is simply for you to use your unique gifts to honor and glorify him.

Lord Jesus, forgive me when I am jealous of what other people have. Help me trust you to meet all my needs. Show me the unique gifts that you have blessed me with and how I can use them to serve you. Amen.

IDOLATRY

All who make idols are nothing, and the things they treasure are worthless. Those who would speak up for them are blind; they are ignorant, to their own shame. . . . This is what the Lord says—your Redeemer, who formed you in the womb: I am the Lord, who has made all things, who alone stretched out the heavens, who spread out the earth by myself. —Isaiah 44:9, 24

Idolatry was a big problem for the nation of Israel. The people would follow God faithfully for a while; but, invariably, hard times would come, and they would create with their own hands a god that they could see—just as all the nations around them had done. At first you might think, "How silly. Why would you worship something you carved out of wood?" But dig a little deeper. What things have you been worshiping besides God lately? Money, popularity, good looks, sports, straight A's? These are all things that we try to make with our own hands and our own efforts, and they can distract us from God in a big way—just as Israel's idols distracted them. Isaiah's words remind us that all our hope, security, and love are rooted in the Lord, who is both the Almighty Creator and our loving Redeemer. Trusting in anything else for meaning and fulfillment gets us nowhere.

God, I know that you want to be first in my life. Forgive me when I worship other things or people instead of you. Show me that true meaning, security, and fulfillment are found only in you. Amen.

PEER PRESSURE

But they would not listen and were as stiff-necked as their fathers, who did not trust in the Lord their God. They rejected his decrees and the covenant he had made with their fathers and the warnings he had given them. They followed worthless idols and themselves became worthless. They imitated the nations around them although the Lord had ordered them, "Do not do as they do," and they did the things the Lord had forbidden them to do. —2 Kings 17:14-15

Israel's problem with idols was also a problem with giving into peer pressure. In this passage, the main mistakes the people made were their rejection of God's ways and their imitation of sinful nations around them. Imagine that your life were being broadcast for millions of people to see, similar to the characters on *The Truman Show* or *EdTV*. What would you want to hide from viewers? The message from this passage is this: If the people around you are doing things that the Lord has said are wrong, do not do as they do.

Name the top three things that tempt you. When and where are these temptations greatest? How can you avoid them? If you feel you can't avoid the situations that tempt you, what do you need to ask the Holy Spirit for so that you may deal with the temptations? Now, think of all the settings where you can find *positive* peer pressure, particularly from other Christians.

> Holy Lord, help me see your ways clearly. Fill me with the desire to honor you with everything that I think and do. Show me how your truth differs so much from the lies and the wrongs I see and hear every day. Amen.

 JANUARY 16

ADDICTED TO WHAT?

Who has woe? Who has sorrow? Who has strife? Who has complaints? Who has needless bruises? Who has bloodshot eyes? Those who linger over wine. . . . In the end it bites like a snake and poisons like a viper. —Proverbs 23:29, 30a, 32

This writer knew all about addiction (read verses 29-35). Perhaps you're addicted to something—drugs, inhalants, cigarettes, alcohol, sex, the computer, or the idea of having a boyfriend/girlfriend. Whatever it is, talk to God about it. Whenever we care about something or someone else more than we care about God and trust God to meet our needs, that thing or person becomes an idol; and we need the help of the Holy Spirit to get our focus back on God.

How we spend our time indicates where our priorities are. If your idol is harmful or wrong, ask the Holy Spirit to enable you to give it up; then seek counseling if needed. If your idol is a good thing that you have taken to extremes, consider a one-week fast from the activity or person. Spend the time you used to give to your idol on a constructive alternative such as Bible study, homework, or time with your family.

> Dear God, thank you for loving and accepting me completely. Help me to trust you to meet all of my needs. When I'm tempted to look at earthly things to find security and acceptance, guide my steps back to the path of your love and righteousness. Amen.

PURITY

Flee from sexual immorality. All other sins a [person] commits are outside [the] body, but [one] who sins sexually sins against his [or her] own body. Do you not know that your body is a temple of the Holy Spirit, who is in you, whom you have received from God? You are not your own; you were bought at a price. Therefore honor God with your body.
—1 Corinthians 6:18-20

Compare Paul's message here with the sexual attitudes in your favorite three TV shows. The phrase "sexual immorality" refers to any sexual activity outside of marriage. In Matthew 5:27-28, Jesus taught that if you even look at another person lustfully, you already have committed sin in your heart—very high standards, indeed, which today would include pornography as well as sexually-oriented sites and chat rooms on the Web.

Paul says, "You are not your own; you were bought at a price." As Christians, we belong to Christ, and he is the one who paid the ultimate price for our sins. How does knowing this motivate you to honor God with your body? Paul also says that our bodies are temples of the Holy Spirit. Could you use a little housecleaning by the Holy Spirit?

Holy Spirit, I want you to live within me. Please cleanse me from any sexual sin—whether in thought, word, or deed—that is keeping me from being a temple of purity for you. Amen.

THE TRUTH ABOUT SEX

Marriage should be honored by all, and the marriage bed kept pure, for God will judge the adulterer and all the sexually immoral.
—Hebrews 13:4

Hollywood promotes an image of sex without consequences—without disease, unwanted pregnancy, or emotional consequences. This is one big, fat, hairy lie! It only takes one sexual encounter to get pregnant or to get a sexually-transmitted disease. These diseases are often painful and can have serious consequences, including infertility and death. Sex outside of marriage has a bunch of emotional consequences, too, including big-time feelings of rejection that lower your self-esteem and interfere with your ability to make a commitment to a lifelong partner.

Another popular misconception is that sex is something you perfect by experimenting with different partners. Here again, things are not as they seem on TV and in movies. The truth is, sex is most fulfilling, enjoyable, and meaningful within marriage. Great sex is rooted in the trust, commitment, and love that two people build within marriage.

Heavenly Father, thank you for the gift of sexual intimacy and for your design of expressing it within marriage. Help me trust that as my Creator, you know what is best for me. Instead of focusing on the physical relationship that I can't have now, help me find ways to make the most of the time I have to serve you and grow closer to you. Amen.

REAL LOVE

Love is patient, love is kind. It does not envy, it does not boast, it is not proud. It is not rude, it is not self-seeking, it is not easily angered, it keeps no record of wrongs. Love does not delight in evil but rejoices with the truth. It always protects, always trusts, always hopes, always perseveres. —*1 Corinthians 13:4-7*

This kind of love is enough to send chills up your spine! God's unconditional, everlasting love for us is almost beyond imagining. This passage also describes the kind of love that the Lord wants us to share with one another in all of our relationships—in our churches, families, friendships, and romantic relationships. We cannot love this way through our own efforts, but the Holy Spirit works in us to transform our hearts so that we may love others as God loves them.

Compare the way Paul describes love in this passage with the kind of love described in this week's top 20 countdown. Where do the popular love songs' portrayals of love fall short of Paul's barometer—in patience, trust, perseverance, and so forth? Use Paul's description of love as a barometer for your own relationships with family and friends. Of the characteristics that Paul describes, which ones are your weakest?

Dear God, thank you for your precious, unconditional love. Thank you for sending Jesus to teach us how to love, and thank you for the ultimate sacrifice he made to show us how much you love us. Fill my heart with your amazing love, and give me opportunities to share it with others. Amen.

STANDING FIRM

So, if you think you are standing firm, be careful that you don't fall! No temptation has seized you except what is common to [everyone]. And God is faithful; he will not let you be

tempted beyond what you can bear. But when you are tempted, he will also provide a way out so that you can stand up under it.
—*1 Corinthians 10:12-13*

Paul warns us that no matter how strong we think we are, we are always susceptible to temptation. The good news is that no one is alone in this battle; everyone faces temptation, and God is faithful to stand by each of us and help us through it. The advice here applies to *anything* that tempts us.

Set your boundaries based on what Jesus would do, especially when it's easy to escape punishment by deceiving your parents about what you're doing. For example, on the Web, avoid sites related to pornography and chat rooms that discuss sex—adults who sexually abuse young people prey on these places and often lie about their identity. Identify whatever really tempts you, and establish what your limits are *before* you get into a sticky situation. Ask a trusted friend to hold you accountable.

Lord, grant me strength to face the temptations of today. Guide me through each situation, and show me the way out of each temptation. Amen.

THE WAY

Jesus answered, "I am the way and the truth and the life. No one comes to the Father except through me." —*John 14:6*

Today, most people define truth by how they *feel* about the issue in question. In contrast, the Bible lays out absolute truths about the nature of God, the nature of people, and the relationship between God and people. Here, Jesus didn't say he was just "a way" or "a source of truth." In essence he was saying, "I am the only way to God the Father; I am the absolute truth that saves you from sin and provides you with salvation; and I am the source of all life." Jesus' bold statement demands that we choose: He is who he said he was, or he was crazy!

If you or your friends struggle with the idea that all religions lead to God and it doesn't matter what you believe as long as you're sincere, read the rest of the book of John. What evidence do you find that points to Jesus as God's Son, in whom we find salvation?

Lord Jesus, open my eyes and my heart to who you really are. When I read your Word, reveal yourself to me, and open my heart to accept you. Amen.

JANUARY 22

APART FROM ME THERE IS NO SAVIOR

"You are my witnesses," declares the Lord, "and my servant whom I have chosen, so that you may know and believe me and understand that I am he. Before me no god was formed, nor will there be one after me. I, even I, am the Lord, and apart from me there is no savior."

—Isaiah 43:10-11

The popular belief that "no religion is always true for everyone" isn't really new. In a way, it is similar to the nation of Israel's tendency to worship idols in Old Testament days. At times the people worshiped gods they thought were powerful and might save them from trouble. If one god is good, they thought, then having several on your side must be even better.

The truth is that it's hopeless to trust in anyone or anything besides the Lord. In both the Old and the New Testaments, we find exclusive claims about God and his plan of salvation. We may reject God and his authority over our lives, but that does not mean God ceases to exist. Nor does it destroy what he has done through Christ. We do not define reality and truth. That's a job for the Creator of the universe.

Why do you think so many people find it hard to acknowledge God and his authority over our lives?

Lord, thank you for providing a simple, clear route to salvation. Forgive us when we don't recognize you as our Creator and Redeemer. When we are tempted to think that it's not fair to make Jesus the only way to you, remind us how unfair it was for us to crucify your only Son when he had committed no sin. Amen.

JANUARY 23

LIVING LIFE TO THE FULL

"The thief comes only to steal and kill and destroy; I have come that they may have life, and have it to the full."   *—John 10:10*

Christianity is not about a set of rules, a list of do's and don'ts. It's about an amazing relationship with our Lord and Savior, Jesus Christ. When we receive his love, forgiveness, and gift of eternal life, everything else falls into place. Out of our gratitude, we seek to honor God in everything.

The boundaries that God sets on our behavior and values may look restrictive to non-Christians. But in reality, God's limits are like the pavement markings and signs on interstate roads. They show us where to drive and how to get where we're going; they don't confine us in a way that's frustrating or difficult. Similarly, living within God's boundaries gives us a full, rich life because we are living according to our Creator's plan. This is how the psalmist could say, "Direct me in the path of your commands, for there I find delight" (Psalm 119:35).

Lord Jesus, thank you for the joy of knowing your love and the blessings you fill my life with. Fill me now with your purpose—to bring you glory and to bring others into a relationship with you. Amen.

JANUARY 24 GOD HATES VIOLENCE

Now the earth was corrupt in God's sight and was full of violence. God saw how corrupt the earth had become, for all the people on earth had corrupted their ways. So God said to Noah, "I am going to put an end to all people, for the earth is filled with violence because of them. I am surely going to destroy both them and the earth." —Genesis 6:11-13

After this statement, God gives Noah instructions for building the ark and uses the flood to wipe out all life on the earth except the people and other living creatures on the ark. Sounds somewhat extreme. But God's actions show how much he hates violence.

Wait a minute, you say. *Doesn't the Old Testament contain a lot of violent stuff?* Yes. Biblical violence falls into two main categories. First there is the violence of wars that God led his chosen people through so that they might take possession of the Promised Land. That is portrayed as a necessary step in establishing the nation of Israel. But the second main category of violence in the Old Testament is plain old sin—caused by people who disobeyed God and mistreated one another.

Think of your favorite video games, movies, web sites, TV shows, music/music videos, and books. Do they convey or promote any violent messages? Do these messages dishonor God? Why or why not?

Sovereign Lord, I praise you because you love justice and you have created me to serve you in righteousness. Sometimes I don't think much about the violent things that I see on TV or hear on the radio because I think that they don't affect me. Show me how to fill my mind and heart with things that honor you and lead to peace. Amen.

JANUARY 25

GIVE UP YOUR VIOLENCE

This is what the Sovereign Lord says: You have gone far enough, O princes of Israel! Give up your violence and oppression and do what is just and right. Stop dispossessing my people, declares the Sovereign Lord.
—Ezekiel 45:9

This verse applies most directly to economic and social injustice—when the rich are unfair to the poor and powerless. But the call to "give up your violence . . . and do what is just and right" also applies to each of us personally.

Think again about your favorite video games, movies, web sites, TV shows, music/music videos, and books. Is violence a common theme? If so, perhaps you feel an adrenaline rush with each video game villain you destroy. Maybe you listen to gangsta rap or heavy metal to vent anger and frustration. Unfortunately, these motives are never satisfied by violent media. The more you listen to violent music, play violent video games, or watch violent movies, the more you crave them and the more desensitized to their violence you become. What can you do instead that honors God?

If violence is not a "common theme," don't congratulate yourself too quickly. Take a closer look to see if any of your favorite pastimes includes secondary or "hidden" images or messages of violence that you may have overlooked. Unfortunately, most of us have become more desensitized to the violence we see and hear about every day than we would like to admit. How may God be calling you to respond?

Sovereign Lord, you call us to give up violence and to do what is just and right instead. Give me a discerning eye when I watch TV or movies, listen to music, play video games, surf the Web, and read so that I may become more aware of the violence. Fill my mind with the good stuff that builds your kingdom. Amen.

JANUARY 26

RACISM

In Christ Jesus you are all children of God through faith. As many of you as were baptized into Christ have clothed yourselves with Christ. There is no longer Jew or Greek, there is no longer slave or free, there is no longer male and female; for all of you are one in Christ Jesus.
—Galatians 3:26-28 (NRSV)

Despite significant improvements in race relations in the United States since the 1960s, racial prejudice remains a deep-rooted weed that chokes human souls. One major cause for concern is the growing number of hate group sites on the Web. Paul makes it clear that we all are the same in God's eyes. In these verses, he is particularly concerned that there be no divisions among Christians.

The people the Jews looked down on in Jesus' day included Samaritans, tax collectors, Roman soldiers, non-Jews, and women. Jesus broke down these barriers. He ate with tax collectors (Luke 5:27-32), taught women (John 4:1-26; Luke 10:38-42), and healed non-Jews (Matthew 15:21-28).

In your use of the Web and other technologies that you know more about than your parents do, set your boundaries based on what Jesus would do. Look up the context of any Bible verses hate groups may use to justify their beliefs, and find where they've gone wrong.

Jesus, thank you for being a fantastic example of how we should treat one another. Give us the kind of sacrificial love that you showed on the cross. May your Spirit urge us to test everything we see against the Bible's teaching. Amen.

LOOKING AT THE HEART

But the LORD said to Samuel, "Do not look on his appearance or on the height of his stature, because I have rejected him [Jesse's oldest son, Eliab]; for the LORD does not see as mortals see; they look on the outward appearance, but the LORD looks on the heart." —1 Samuel 16:7 (NRSV)

This is an excellent example of how God values the opposite of what we value. In 1 Samuel 16:1-13, we read how the prophet Samuel anointed David to be Israel's future king. David was the youngest of eight sons, a mere shepherd boy. At this point, he had done nothing noteworthy. But, looking at David's heart instead of his outward appearance, God saw his potential and chose him.

What do the people who appear on magazine covers and in TV ads look like? Ninety-nine percent are thin; and they have perfect skin, beautiful hairstyles, and great clothes. Our culture idolizes youth and physical beauty. It's no wonder so many people struggle with eating disorders and/or spend hours working out in the gym—beyond what's needed for physical fitness. Guess what? God doesn't care how you *look*. God loves you for who you *are*, and God made you that way for a purpose.

Dear God, thank you for loving me from the inside out. Show me how to be comfortable with how you made me—with my looks, personality, and talents. Teach me not to look at the outward appearance but at the heart. Amen.

JANUARY 28

GOD'S IDEAL WOMAN

A wife of noble character who can find? She is worth far more than rubies . . . She is clothed with strength and dignity . . . She speaks with wisdom, and faithful instruction is on her tongue . . . Charm is deceptive and beauty is fleeting; but a woman who fears the LORD is to be praised.
—Proverbs 31:10, 25a, 26, 30

If aliens visited earth and saw our movies, romance novels, magazines, and TV shows, what kind of woman would they think earthlings value? They'd probably say, "As long as she's pretty and thin, not much else matters."

How does God's ideal woman in Proverbs 31:10-31 differ from the world's ideal woman? The proverb never once says anything about looks or popularity. Instead, it concentrates on her character and how it is reflected in her actions. Charm and beauty aren't what matters. The woman who reveres God and pursues a life of righteousness is the one who's worthy of praise.

This proverb has great significance for both guys and gals. Gals, here's a *real* model to follow—not some crazy super model image. Guys, what you see with your eyes is not nearly as important as what lies below the surface.

Thanks for showing us how to look below the surface to see what's really valuable in a person, God. Please put at least one person in my path today who isn't good-looking or popular, and give me the courage to become that person's friend. Amen.

JANUARY 29

GOD'S LOVE

For I am convinced that neither death nor life, neither angels nor demons, neither the present nor the future, nor any powers, neither height nor depth, nor anything else in all creation, will be able to separate us from the love of God that is in Christ Jesus our Lord.
—Romans 8:38-39

"I am nothing without you." "My life has no meaning without you." Most of us wouldn't say these things in ordinary conversation, but we listen to them every day in the lyrics of popular music played on the radio. Popular culture deceives us into thinking these messages are true about *people*, but actually they're statements we can only make about *God*. Romantic love is wonderful, but nothing fills the gaping void inside each of us like the Lord Jesus Christ. Other people do provide meaning in our lives, but our deepest needs for love, acceptance, and meaning can only be met by

God. God's the only one you can *always* count on. Plus, you have value simply because God created you in his image, and God called everything he made "very good" (Genesis 1:27, 31). You are completely loved by God as his child, made in his image—whether or not you ever have a date!

What amazing love you have lavished on us, Lord! You created us in your image. You sent your Son to give us hope for our lives in this world and the next. You heal all our hurts with your perfect love. Thank you! Amen.

NEW SPIRIT, NEW HEART

I will give you a new heart and put a new spirit in you; I will remove from you your heart of stone and give you a heart of flesh. And I will put my Spirit in you and move you to follow my decrees and be careful to keep my laws. —Ezekiel 36:26-27

We have looked at many issues this month. What areas in popular culture are the biggest challenges for you? Ask the Holy Spirit to show you which of your values are shaped more by the world than by the Lord. It's not about giving something up. It's about God changing your heart so that you long to honor and bring glory to God in all you think and do.

God makes some key points in the verses preceding this passage from Ezekiel. In spite of all the stuff Israel had done to dishonor God, God would forgive them and give them a new spirit and a new heart to follow him— simply for the sake of his holy name. Then the world would know he really is God, and they'd see his holiness through Israel's changed hearts and lives (see verses 22-23). God longs to do the same thing through our lives today.

Sovereign Lord, put your Spirit in me and move me to follow your righteous ways. Change my heart so that other people may see you in me and believe. Amen.

SETTING THE EXAMPLE

Don't let anyone look down on you because you are young, but set an example for the believers in speech, in life, in love, in faith and in purity. —1 Timothy 4:12

What are your life goals? How does your faith in Christ shape those goals?

Paul's goal was to know Jesus Christ and to make him known to others (see Philippians 3:10 and Ephesians 1:17). The psalms are full of encouragement to glorify God—to make him look good to others; to praise and honor him. In the end, these are the only things that matter, and they are God's purpose for our lives. This is why we need to distinguish the differences between God's values and the world's values. God wants us to fill our minds and hearts with things that honor and glorify him. He wants us to be temples of the Holy Spirit, so that his light might shine through us and draw others to him. And best of all, God will do all of this through us, no matter how young we are, if we allow his Spirit to work through us!

Holy God, may my faith and my life make others excited to know you. Use my life to shine your light before others and draw them to you. Amen.

FEBRUARY

ONE OF THE GREATEST LETTERS EVER WRITTEN

Ken and Liz Carter

ONE OF THE GREATEST LETTERS EVER WRITTEN

Ken and Liz Carter

CHRISTIAN FRIENDS

I thank my God . . . because of your partnership in the gospel from the first day until now. . . . I have you in my heart; for . . . all of you share in God's grace with me. —Philippians 1:3, 5, 7

This month we will be reading portions of one of the greatest letters ever written, a letter written by the apostle Paul to the Christians in Philippi. This letter communicates joy in the midst of suffering and calls us to be servants of Jesus against great odds. We hope you'll feel as if Paul is writing this letter to you, today!

There was a partnership between Paul and the Philippians. These friends gave Paul the strength to accomplish God's purpose for his life, which was to share the good news about Jesus with the whole world. As you seek to discover and accomplish God's purpose for *your* life, remember that you are never alone. There are partners, both seen and unseen, who share God's grace with you. You may feel isolated from other Christians; Paul was in prison when he wrote these words. Or you may be surrounded by others who strengthen your faith. In either case, think about one or two Christian friends who have made a difference in your life, and give thanks to God for them today.

God, I thank you for friends who strengthen my faith, who help me to fulfill your purpose for my life. Amen.

A WORK IN PROGRESS

He who began a good work in you will carry it on to completion until the day of Christ Jesus. —Philippians 1:6

Being a Christian is a journey. You begin—you take steps—day by day. You make progress. But sometimes you feel as if you are moving backward, the winds blowing against you. You get discouraged. You wonder if you should keep going or if you will make it.

Paul's words remind you that God walks with you and that God will help you to make it. God is faithful. God will finish the work begun in you. When you follow Jesus, you still have good days and bad days. The only constant is a simple truth: "He who began a good work in you will carry it on to completion until the day of Christ Jesus." Today, memorize three simple words: God is faithful!

I thank you, God, for the promise that you will complete all that you have started to do in my life. Amen.

GIVING YOUR BEST TO GOD

This is my prayer . . . that you may be able to discern what is best and may be pure and blameless until the day of Christ.
—*Philippians 1:9-10*

The Bible teaches about the judgment of God. God's judgments are always fair, always truthful, always a part of God's plan. Many of the parables of Jesus are about judgment, such as the parable of the sheep and the goats in Matthew 25. Judgment reminds us that we are accountable to God. We owe our lives to God. God has given us every good thing that we have: our time, our talents, our material possessions.

God has placed something in your hands, something that you might share with others, something that you might return to God. On the day of judgment, God will ask how you have taken the blessings and multiplied them. On that day you will be accountable to God.

How can you give your best to God today?

God, today I give you all that I am and all that I have. Amen.

ROOTED IN THE SOIL OF FAITH

Filled with the fruit of righteousness that comes through Jesus Christ—to the glory and praise of God. —*Philippians 1:11*

The Bible is rich with images of growth and harvest, often speaking of God's attentiveness, patience, and timing. Just as we depend on the soil for food and for life itself, so also we depend on God, who creates, nurtures, and sustains. To "bear fruit" is to be a part of a miracle that God makes possible. Remember that you are connected to Jesus the way a branch is connected to a vine. As you grow stronger in faith, you will bear fruit; you will become the person you were created to be. God has a plan for your life and will give you the means to accomplish it. Even when you deviate from the plan, God can make it work.

When something is planted, there is the hope that someday it will bear fruit. God created you. God's hope is that you will glorify him in your life.

O God, let me become more rooted in the soil of faith, and let my life glorify you. Amen.

BEING A WITNESS

Now I want you to know . . . that what has happened to me has really served to advance the gospel. —Philippians 1:12

Have you ever been unjustly accused or unfairly punished for something? Paul was in prison because of his witness for the Christian faith. How did he respond? He said that his imprisonment had helped others to know about Jesus and that his strength had encouraged others.

The Letter to the Philippians is filled with joy and encouragement. Remember that Paul's circumstances weren't always joyful and encouraging, but his inner strength helped him to see beyond the chains that imprisoned him. You can have that same inner strength, even when you are unjustly accused or unfairly punished. And your responses to hard times may help to advance the gospel, just as Paul's did.

> At the end of a long, dark tunnel,
>   you can always see the light;
> even when times are getting rough,
>   hope will still burn bright.
> —Liz Carter

O God, today help me to be a witness, even when life is difficult. Amen.

CHOICES

For to me, to live is Christ and to die is gain.
—Philippians 1:21

Your life is filled with choices, decisions, dilemmas. You have been placed on this earth by God, and yet you also have been filled with a desire to live in God's presence. As you become a more mature follower of Jesus, you will know that God's presence is possible in life and in death.

In a memorial service we attended, these words were prayed:

> Help us to live as those who are prepared to die.
> And when our days here are accomplished,
>   enable us to die as those who go forth to live,
>   so that living or dying, our life may be in you.
>
> (From "A Service of Death and Resurrection,"
> *The United Methodist Hymnal*, © 1989 The United
> Methodist Publishing House)

Have you been putting off something that is important to you—maybe something you feel God is calling you to do? Live in God's presence today, and do what is most important.

God, let me live today in your presence, and guide me to what is most important. Amen.

 # STAND FIRM

Whatever happens, conduct yourselves in a manner worthy of the gospel of Christ . . . without being frightened in any way by those who oppose you.   —Philippians 1:27-28a

When you follow Jesus, sometimes you feel odd or unusual. You may not fit in with everything that happens around you. This was true in the first century, and it is true in the twenty-first century.

Have you ever taken a stand against something, or a stand in support of something, because of your faith? Can you think of groups or behaviors that "oppose you" as a follower of Jesus? What do you think it means to conduct yourself "in a manner worthy of the gospel of Christ"? How would your life be different if you lived each day this way?

Paul gave a simple command: Stand firm (v. 27). At times you will feel odd or unusual or different. But remember that you are following Jesus, and that is what matters!

O God, give me the strength and the confidence to follow Jesus today. Amen.

FEBRUARY 8 SUFFERING

It has been granted to you on behalf of Christ not only to believe on him, but also to suffer for him. —Philippians 1:29

Imagine that someone is selling you a product, and the salesperson makes it seem amazing and precious. How honest or how disclosing do you think the person is being?

Paul was "selling" the Philippians on being a follower of Jesus, yet he was straightforward and completely honest. Being a believer can bring comfort and hope and joy, but believing in Jesus also can bring suffering.

One of the most important truths for a young person who wants to follow Jesus is this: The road will not always be smooth; the experiences will not always be fun. At those times when the road is rough, remember the road upon which Jesus walked when he carried the cross. He has known what it is like to suffer and to be tempted. Today he walks with you.

> *After wounding sorrows,*
> *joys always appear;*
> *after the sun has risen,*
> *stars are always near.*
> —Liz Carter

God, today help me to encourage and pray for someone who is suffering. Amen.

FEBRUARY 9 LOVING OTHERS

If you have any encouragement from being united with Christ, if any comfort from his love, if any fellowship from his Spirit, if any tenderness and compassion, then make my joy complete by being like-minded, having the same love, being one in spirit and purpose. —Philippians 2:1-2

As you follow Jesus, you will discover that others are walking the same road. Sometimes this will seem wonderful—you're not alone. At other times it will cause new problems, because some of those followers of Jesus will be people with whom you don't get along or agree. You might not even like them! But remember: Whatever faults they have, you might have an equal number. Jesus taught us to remove the plank from our own eyes before we worry too much about the speck in our neighbor's eye (Matthew 7:3-5). He also instructed us, "Love each other, as I have loved you" (John 15:12 CEV). It's easy to love Jesus, but sometimes it's hard to love each other.

Paul knew all about this. "Make my joy complete," he wrote, "by . . .

being one in spirit and purpose." He insisted that being a follower of Jesus means becoming more compassionate to others, especially those who need it the most. One of the tests of being a Christian is how we love one another. Are you passing the test?

Lord, let me love someone today, remembering that you first loved me. Amen.

HUMILITY

In humility consider others better than yourselves.
—*Philippians 2:3*

In the world, we strive for first place, not second. We want to go to the best school. We want to win. We want the advantage. We want to sit in the best seat, closer to the front. We want to drive the fastest car.

Following Jesus changes all of that. Let today's scripture be a challenge for you. Would you consider: letting someone go before you in a restaurant? giving someone the parking place you have been waiting for? helping someone who is not as accomplished as you in a sport or other activity? tutoring someone to learn material that you've already mastered? Can you put yourself in the place of someone who will lose at something today?

Jesus modeled humility. For your sake, he gave his life. As you follow him, you will learn more about humility.

Lord, help me to practice humility in some specific, concrete way today. Amen.

BEING A SERVANT

Your attitude should be the same as that of Christ Jesus: Who, being in the very nature of God, did not consider equality with God something to be grasped, but made himself nothing, taking the very nature of a servant.
—*Philippians 2:5-7*

Jesus gave up everything because of his love for the world. When he entered the world, he gave up his divine status (equality with God) and emptied himself. Although he was God, he became a servant.

The story is familiar: A child is born into a royal family and is kidnapped. The child does hard labor and eventually winds up working for the royal family. When the true identity of the child is discovered, the child becomes the new ruler of the kingdom.

Jesus gave up royalty to become a slave. He was God, but he voluntarily assumed the lowest form of humanity. He emptied himself and willingly became nothing. He gave up everything—his position, his comfort—and he suffered and died *for us.*

We do not have to search for God. God comes to us in Jesus the servant. Look around: Do you see him?

Lord, today help me to discover you among those I serve. Amen.

FEBRUARY 12 GOD IS IN CONTROL

Therefore God exalted him to the highest place and gave him the name that is above every name. —Philippians 2:9

God is a God of surprises. God is a God of reversals. Where there is self-emptying, there is exaltation. With death, there is resurrection. What seems to be lowly, God has a marvelous way of lifting up. Look up the parable of the pharisee and the tax collector in Luke 18.

When you think everything is totally out of control, remember that God is in control. When you think evil has the upper hand, remember that God loves surprises and that, ultimately, justice triumphs. When you think you cannot be any lower, remember that God can give you a peace that cannot be explained.

We were driving through a rural area once and came upon a sign outside a small country church that read: "When you realize that God is all you have, God is all you need!" God is love, and, as the Beatles sang, "all you need is love."

God of power and might, help me to be open to the surprises you have in store for me today. Amen.

FEBRUARY 13 JESUS IS LORD OF ALL

At the name of Jesus every knee should bow, in heaven and on earth and under the earth, and every tongue confess that Jesus Christ is Lord, to the glory of God the Father. —Philippians 2:10-11

Jesus is interested in every part of your life—how you spend your money, how you treat your friends, how you use your mind, how you take care of your body. You may think a certain sin is too small to matter to him, but sin has no size. To confess Jesus as Lord is to allow him to direct all your thoughts and actions, to place him at the center of your life, to become obedient to him.

Because Jesus was obedient, God has exalted him. His name is above every name. As you look to him for strength and guidance today, you might find a quiet, private place and position yourself on your knees. As you kneel before Jesus, quietly, in your own words and in your own way, say to him, "You are the Lord of all creation. You are my Lord. I give my life to you."

Lord, today I will reflect on your greatness. Amen.

 # SALVATION

Therefore, my dear friends, as you have always obeyed—not only in my presence, but now much more in my absence—continue to work out your own salvation with fear and trembling, for it is God who works in you to will and to act according to his good purpose.
—Philippians 2:12-13

God has given you a wonderful gift: salvation. But you have to work with it, discover what it means, come to an acceptance of it. That is your free will, which also is a gift from God.

Have you ever received a gift that was so amazing or surprising that you felt a lump forming in your throat and your knees getting weak? The gift of salvation is something that creates awe and trembling. You might wonder: *What did I do to deserve such an incredible gift?* The answer is *nothing*. You don't earn the gift of salvation, but you do have a part in it as you live out your salvation.

God's salvation is given to those who devote themselves to it. The good news is that God is working in you, helping you to do things beyond your power.

God, continue your work of salvation in me. Amen.

 # THE "WORD OF LIFE"

As you hold out the word of life—in order that I may boast on the day of Christ that I did not run or labor for nothing.
—Philippians 2:16

Paul evaluated his success as a servant of God on the basis of the faithfulness of his friends, the Philippians. What had they done with the gift of salvation that God had given to them?

The "word of life" Paul referred to is Jesus. Paul was saying that if the Philippians would stay close to Jesus, they also would reveal to others who

Jesus is by their words and by their actions. If the Philippians would draw strength from Jesus, the word of life, they would remain faithful.

Perhaps you can think of a youth counselor, a Sunday school teacher, a Scout leader, or a pastor who has affected your life. The test of whether this person's work on this earth has been worthwhile will be in how you—and others like you—hold on to the word of life, Jesus Christ.

Lord, today help me to stay close to you, and help others to see your presence in my life. Amen.

MOTIVATIONS

I hope in the Lord Jesus to send Timothy to you soon, that I also may be cheered when I receive news about you. I have no one else like him, who takes a genuine interest in your welfare. For everyone looks out for his [or her] own interests, not those of Jesus Christ.
—Philippians 2:19-21

Motivations are important. The end does not justify the means. A worthy purpose does not justify questionable actions. Followers of Jesus are to practice the gospel in ways that reflect the gospel.

Have you ever started with good intentions and ended up in a mess? It helps to constantly examine our motives and ask ourselves, "Why am I doing this?" Even servants of God can be looking out primarily for their own interests.

Timothy's motivations were in the right place. For this reason, Paul asked him to perform a very important task. Paul trusted Timothy because he was a person of character.

Remember, God looks not only at the end result but also at the motivation behind it. Can you think of a way you have been sidetracked? Can you ask God to take away a false motive so that you can be a more faithful servant?

Lord, I do the right things, but not always for the right reasons. I ask your forgiveness. Amen.

SOMETHING EVEN BETTER

Whatever was to my profit I now consider loss for the sake of Christ. What is more, I consider everything a loss compared to the surpassing greatness of knowing Christ Jesus my Lord. *—Philippians 3:7-8*

Sometimes a person will share a testimony about how low he or she had sunk in life before receiving God's grace. Paul's story was just the opposite. He had everything—born into an elite family with all the advantages—and he always had followed the rules. No one was more religious or righteous than Paul. Yet Paul gave all of this up in order to know Jesus Christ as his Lord.

Sometimes God calls weak people and makes them strong. But sometimes God calls strong people and asks them to give up their strengths in order to receive something even better.

Has your own life been like Paul's? Maybe you have a long list of accomplishments that are pretty important to you. Are they more important than knowing Jesus Christ as your Lord? How would you write the story of your life?

God, today, if I am strong, show me the surpassing greatness of knowing Jesus. Amen.

KNOWING JESUS

I want to know Christ and the power of his resurrection and the fellowship of sharing in his sufferings, becoming like him in his death. —*Philippians 3:10*

There is a difference between knowing about someone and actually knowing someone. To know Jesus Christ is more than knowing about him—where he lived, what he did, what he said. To know Jesus Christ is to be changed by the power of his resurrection. To know Jesus Christ is to receive a faith that overcomes sin and death and brings you to eternal life. To know Jesus Christ also is to come under the shadow of the cross. Sometimes you will carry heavy burdens and endure pain and suffering. But the resurrection power of Jesus will strengthen you—in the present and in the future. And the fellowship of Jesus' suffering will make you more aware of how others are hurting.

So—how well do you know Jesus?

God, I ask not that I would know more about Jesus; help me to *know* Jesus. Amen.

RESURRECTION

And so, somehow, to attain to the resurrection from the dead. —*Philippians 3:11*

Have you ever lost someone close to you? Have you ever placed flowers beside a grave or watched someone else do so? When we do that, we are saying, "Yes, there is death, but there also is life!" This belief is crucial to our faith. It all began with Easter.

Easter is not only about Christ's death; it is about Christ's *resurrection* from the dead. Because Christ conquered death, we too may inherit eternal life. Like Paul, we can put our hope in attaining the resurrection from the dead.

Perhaps you have attended an Easter sunrise service. Sunrise services often are held early in the morning. When the sun appears, the night ends. The light shines in the darkness, and a new day begins. Resurrection is about a new beginning, a new life, which begins at death.

To know Jesus is not only to know that he has been raised from the dead; to know Jesus is to be raised from the dead with him!

I thank you, Lord, for the hope you give me in a life beyond death, through Jesus. Amen.

PRESS ON!

Not that I have already obtained all this, or have already been made perfect, but I press on to take hold of that for which Christ Jesus took hold of me. —Philippians 3:12

The Christian life is a pilgrimage. Martin Luther, the great reformer of Christianity, wrote, "We are not yet what we shall be, but we are growing toward it." Paul enjoyed a close relationship with Christ, but he also looked forward to an even deeper relationship.

As a follower of Jesus, you live in this life, but you also look forward, with hope, to the life to come. And if you are honest, you confess with all followers of Jesus that you are not yet perfect.

Today, think about these questions: What progress am I making as a follower of Jesus? In which areas of life do I have a long way to go? Am I sometimes discouraged that I'm not closer to Christ? Remember, following Jesus is a continuing journey. Paul urges you to "press on"!

Today, Lord Jesus, help me to run and not grow weary, to walk and not faint, to keep on trying. Amen.

RUNNING TOWARD THE PRIZE

But one thing I do: Forgetting what is behind and straining toward what is ahead, I press on toward the goal to win the prize for which God has called me heavenward in Christ Jesus. —Philippians 3:13-14

Following Jesus is like being in a race. You can only look forward, toward the finish line. If you look back, you will be slowed down. If you keep your eyes focused on the destination and move toward it, you will complete the race.

You may be thinking about something that has happened in your life, something in the past. Maybe something in your past is a burden to you. Maybe you have walked in directions that took you away from God.

The scripture invites you to forget what is in the past and to run toward the goal that God has for your life. The prize is heaven—a life with the God who created you and loves you, a life that never ends.

Lord, keep me focused on your goal for my life. Amen.

WHOSE EXAMPLE WILL YOU FOLLOW?

Join with others in following my example . . . and take note of those who live according to the pattern we gave you.
—Philippians 3:17

As you make progress in life, look around: You probably didn't get to where you are by yourself. Have you patterned your life after a particular person or group of persons? Are you easily tempted to go along with the unfaithful crowd, or are you committed to following the example of the faithful? And if no one else is faithful, are you willing to be that example for others?

As a follower of Jesus, you are to look to him as your primary example. Get in the habit of asking yourself this familiar question: "What would Jesus do?" You also are blessed with the example of faithful Christians whose lives are worthy of imitation. They strengthen you. They encourage you. They say, by their actions, "I want you to follow me as I follow Jesus." Paul was an example to his friends, the Philippians. Whose example will you follow today? Remember, whether you realize it or not, someone's also following you!

I thank you, Lord, for leading me to persons who are following you. May I also be a good example for others. Amen.

DESTRUCTIVE PATHS

For, as I have often told you before and now say again even with tears, many live as enemies of the cross of Christ. Their destiny is destruction. . . . Their mind is on earthly things. *—Philippians 3:18-19*

We live in a culture filled with compulsive behaviors and destructive activities. You can look around and see that people are obsessed with pleasure; they look for any way possible to satisfy their appetites for what they want at the moment: drugs, sex, money, cars, success, popularity, and so on. "Their destiny," Paul writes, "is destruction."

Do you know someone, perhaps a friend, whose destiny is destruction? Can you offer a prayer for that person now?

You also know that, at times, your mind is on earthly things. Focusing on earthly things is the exact opposite of following Jesus; Paul calls this the destiny of becoming an enemy of the cross.

The cross of Jesus stands in opposition to anything—you can fill in the blank—that seeks to take the place of Jesus. If you are wondering if a particular behavior or decision is destructive, look at a cross. The answer will become clearer to you.

Forgive me, Lord, for the times when I have followed paths that are destructive. Help me to follow you. Amen.

BEING AN ALIEN

Our citizenship is in heaven. And we eagerly await a Savior from there, the Lord Jesus Christ, who, by the power that enables him to bring everything under his control, will transform our lowly bodies so that they will be like his glorious body.
—Philippians 3:20-21

We once heard this saying: "We are not human beings having a spiritual experience. We are spiritual beings having a human experience." Likewise, C. S. Lewis once remarked, "If we aim for heaven, we get earth thrown in with it; if we aim for earth, we get nothing."

The life to come has a profound impact on how followers of Jesus live in the present. The Bible expresses it very simply: God created you. God has a claim upon you. Jesus goes to prepare a place for you.

One of our favorite TV programs is "The X-Files." Agent Mulder is a seeker, convinced that "the truth is out there," and he is sure that aliens inhabit the earth. As a follower of Jesus, you are a citizen of heaven, an alien here on Earth, and your search is always rewarded. You are in touch with the power of God, which overcomes sin and death.

God of power and might, you are above all things, and I belong to you. Thank you! Amen.

CHOOSE JOY

Rejoice in the Lord always. I will say it again: Rejoice!
—Philippians 4:4

Sometimes you have no external reason to be joyful, but remember: Joy is a *choice*.

Paul was in prison. He had no external reason to be joyful. His only reasons for rejoicing were internal. He could rejoice "in the Lord." The Lord, powerful and joyous, was *inside* of Paul!

Take a moment. List all of the external obstacles to joy. Do you feel restricted? accused? labeled? Have you been hurt? blamed? neglected?

Remember: Joy is a choice. Commit Philippians 4:4 to memory. When you feel like you are imprisoned, remember your brother Paul and rejoice. When you feel separated from your friends, remember your brother Paul and rejoice.

There is a reason to choose joy. Paul gives it to us in Philippians 4:5: "The Lord is near." Do not focus on external obstacles that surround you like walls of a prison. Rejoice in the Lord always, who is always near!

Today, Lord, help me to choose joy. Amen.

WORRIES

Do not be anxious about anything, but in everything, by prayer and petition, with thanksgiving, present your requests to God.
—Philippians 4:6

Are you anxious about today—or perhaps tomorrow? Are you worried about school or money or friends? Is there enough time for all that you have to do? Do you feel responsible for problems you didn't create?

As a follower of Jesus, you are not immune from being anxious and worried. At times problems, big and small, overwhelm you. You want to hide or explode or give up.

Paul's letter to the Philippians gives a wonderful prescription for those who are anxious and worried: prayer. When things are out of control, remember to pray for yourself and for others, being as specific as you can and being grateful to God for listening.

Lord, whatever I cannot handle, I will give to you in prayer. Amen.

INCREDIBLE PEACE

And the peace of God, which transcends all understanding, will guard your hearts and your minds in Christ Jesus.
—*Philippians 4:7*

When you are overwhelmed, pray. Something amazing will happen. A peace that you cannot explain will surround you. This peace comes only from God. It is God's way of letting you know that nothing is overwhelming to God. God can handle it. And therefore, so can you! God wants you to receive this gift of peace.

"Do not be anxious about anything . . . present your requests to God. And the peace of God, which transcends all understanding, will guard your hearts and your minds in Christ Jesus" (Philippians 4:6-7). What could make your day more peaceful?

> *I sit at the edge of a rock*
> *bordered by a flowing stream;*
> *I sit there quietly in thought,*
> *I dive into a peaceful dream.*
> —Liz Carter

God, I thank you for Jesus, the prince of peace. Keep me close to him today. Amen.

WHAT'S ON YOUR MIND?

Finally . . . whatever is true, whatever is noble, whatever is right, whatever is pure, whatever is lovely, whatever is admirable—if anything is excellent or praiseworthy—think about such things.
—*Philippians 4:8*

In his letter to the Philippians, Paul encouraged his friends to think about those things that would make their lives more pleasing to God. In their thoughts, speech, and actions, they were to consider what was best.

In your own life, you make the decision to sift between true and false, right and wrong, pure and contaminated, excellent and mediocre. You have many choices.

> *I sift through words and pick a few,*
> *Say them aloud and, beginning anew,*
> *Find some; then, dismissing the rest,*
> *I say the words that I think best.*
> —Liz Carter

What are you thinking about today? What will you think about tomorrow—and the next day, and the next? As you continue life's journey, may you always think about those things that will make your life more pleasing to God.

Lord, may my thoughts and my words always be acceptable to you. Amen.

MARCH

LIFE'S NOT ALWAYS EASY, BUT GOD IS ALWAYS GOOD

Steve Broderson

MARCH

LIFE'S NOT ALWAYS EASY, BUT GOD IS ALWAYS GOOD

Steve Broderson

MARCH

"WHY?"

How long, O God, will our enemies laugh at you?
Will they insult your name forever?
Why have you refused to help us?
Why do you keep your hands behind you?
—*Psalm 74:10-11 (TEV)*

A disturbed student opens fire on a group of his classmates praying together in school. A close friend is killed in a wreck. We hear reports of floods, earthquakes, and killer tornadoes. We don't have to look very far to see tragedy, pain, and death.

It's a question almost as old as creation itself, and one that everyone eventually asks: If there is an all-powerful God, why do bad things happen? How did all this awful, hurtful stuff get into the mix?

We'll be exploring some of these difficult questions this month. These devotions certainly won't answer all your questions; they may even spark new ones. Their purpose is to help you give some serious thought to the issue of pain and suffering. The problem of evil and tragedy can be a big roadblock to your faith and the faith of your friends—that is, unless you are willing to wrestle with some difficult questions that will both challenge and deepen your faith. Then when the inevitable storms of life come, you will be better prepared to withstand them.

Dear Lord, I know bad things happen, and I wonder "Why?" sometimes. I ask your Holy Spirit to help me as I struggle with this question. Amen.

MARCH 2 — IT'S OK TO ASK TOUGH QUESTIONS

My God, my God, why have you abandoned me?
I have cried desperately for help, but it still does not come.
—Psalm 22:1 (TEV)

Wizard: Do not arouse the wrath of the Great and Powerful Oz! I said come back tomorrow!

Dorothy: If you were really great and powerful, you'd keep your promises!

Wizard: Do you presume to criticize the Great Oz? You ungrateful creatures! Think yourselves lucky that I'm giving you an audience tomorrow, instead of twenty years from now! The Great Oz has spoken!

When we ask the question, Why do bad things happen? we can feel like Dorothy asking her simple questions in front of an angry wizard. It's important to realize, though, that God is big enough to handle our questioning. You are not the first to ask "Why?" when things get tough, and you won't be the last. Jesus himself felt abandoned by God as he hung dying on the cross, and he quoted this verse from Psalm 22. The psalms are full of praises, but they also contain anguished cries and accusations toward the Creator. These are not disrespectful taunts; the psalmist is just "getting real" with God. We can and should do the same. This month we're looking at some tough questions on an important subject; don't be afraid to raise your hand in this class!

Dear God, I have lots of questions about pain, suffering, and tragedy. But I know you're big enough to handle my questions. Help me to listen for your voice. Amen.

MARCH 3 — THE SIN VIRUS

It is true that through the sin of one man death began to rule because of that one man. *—Romans 5:17 (TEV)*

When early computer programmers decided to abbreviate years to only two digits, it seemed like a good idea. It would save lots of time and memory. Unfortunately, that decision has had a huge impact on everything that relies on computers: the Year 2000 bug. These small sets of instructions, passed down through hundreds of generations of software, can bring a well-running machine grinding to a halt.

Adam and Eve's first act of disobedience also had a huge ripple effect. God created people to live forever, having all their needs met. Sin changed all that. Not only did people begin to age and die, they had to start hunting and growing their own food just to survive! Rebellion, pain, and death had swan-dived right into our gene pool. Just like those bug-ridden computers, it seems we have a virus hard-wired in our system!

Merciful God, I know that without you I am still in a state of sin and sickness. I know it was not your will for sin to enter the human race, but I ask that you help me daily to overcome this flaw within me, making me a new creature. Amen.

MARCH 4

THE CURE TO SIN'S GRIP

Sin must no longer rule in your mortal bodies so that you obey the desires of your natural self. Nor must you surrender any part of yourselves to sin to be used for wicked purposes. Instead, give yourselves to God, as those who have been brought from death to life, and surrender your whole being to him to be used for righteous purposes. —Romans 6:12, 13 (TEV)

Let's say someone in your youth group or the group you hang with at school has diabetes. It's a lifelong disease, but it can be treated if you take insulin and cut down on sugar. Let's say you see this person at the mall eating all kinds of candy and washing it down with a soft drink. "What are you doing?" you ask. "I thought you were diabetic!" "Yes, I am, and I always will be. So what's your point?" the person asks between bites of caramel corn.

Just recognizing we have sin within us doesn't do us any good unless we do something about it. God has provided a way of treating this disease and its deadly symptoms. Jesus' sacrifice on the cross provided the cure to sin's grip. We don't have to worry about dying from the disease, but we must treat it with daily doses of prayer and God's Word.

Dear Lord, thank you for your one-shot cure for sin. I claim your sacrifice as the cure for my disease, but I ask you for the discipline to keep treating my symptoms. Amen.

MARCH 5

A "DOUBLE-EDGED" GIFT

As for you, my friends, you were called to be free. But do not let this freedom become an excuse for letting your physical desires control you. —Galatians 5:13 (TEV)

WARNING! PRODUCT CONTAINS KNOWLEDGE OF GOOD AND EVIL. IF EATEN, WILL CAUSE DISEASE, PAIN, SEPARATION FROM GOD, AND EVENTUALLY DEATH.

God should have put a warning label on that fruit. As much hurt and suffering as "the knowledge of good and evil" has caused, a tall fence around that tree would have been even better. God must have known people were going to mess things up eventually. Why not just hide it or make it impossible to reach? Why not make "the knowledge of good and evil" unknowable?

Some bad things happen to good people partly because of sin's effect on us—pain, sickness, and ultimately the natural death of the body. But another reason bad things happen is wrapped up in a gift God gave human creations, a gift with a "double edge"—the potential to do great good or great harm: free will.

Heavenly Father, help me discern the pain that was caused by the first sin—and not blame you for it. And help me to use the gift of freedom you have given me wisely. Amen.

MARCH 6 THE CHOICE IS YOURS

"Who told you that you were naked?" God asked. "Did you eat the fruit that I told you not to eat?" The man answered, "The woman you put here with me gave me the fruit, and I ate it." The Lord God asked the woman, "Why did you do this?" She replied, "The snake tricked me into eating it."
—Genesis 3:11-13 (TEV)

"The Devil made me do it!" goes a popular saying. But is that really true? Did Satan make Eve disobey God? Did Satan then force Adam to try the fruit? For that matter, does Satan have the power to *make* us do anything? Not according to Scripture. The serpent sold those first humans on the idea, but it was Adam and Eve who made the decision to eat the fruit. A choice was made. Boom. Sin entered in. But it didn't stop there. It spread.

Adam and Eve's son Able was a good man, and God loved him. But Able had a brother, Cain, who became jealous of Able and killed him. Did God want this to happen? Where was God when Cain was about to strike? Why didn't God prevent this tragedy?

Cain exercised his free will and *chose* to kill. Sometimes the bad things that happen to us result from the free will acts of ourselves and others.

Lord, I know Satan has no power over me, except what I allow. Help me to know when I'm being lied to, and give me the strength to resist evil and do what is right. Amen.

MARCH 7 — USING YOUR FREEDOM RESPONSIBLY

I am now giving you a choice between life and death, between God's blessing and God's curse, and I call heaven and earth to witness the choice you make. Choose life. —Deuteronomy 30:19 (TEV)

Ever seen a dog wake up one morning and decide it's pointless to continue chasing squirrels? Or what about a cat decide it's going to eat less in order to lose weight? Animals don't have the gift of free will which God gave all people. God decided we would be set apart from the animals. We can make choices about our behavior instead of "running on instinct."

This "double-edged" gift means that if we choose to, we can disobey or even reject God. Unfortunately, there are many people who choose to do just that. God wants each of us to freely love our Creator; but in giving us this freedom, God also takes a huge risk. Because God is not a "puppet master," we often choose to do evil, hurtful things to ourselves and to others.

Dear God, thank you for the gift of free will. I want to use my freedom to return your love—not to rebel against you. Help me to be responsible with my freedom. Amen.

MARCH 8 — NATURAL CONSEQUENCES

If you refuse good advice, you are asking for trouble; follow it and you are safe. —Proverbs 13:13 (TEV)

"Put your shoes on, Alaina. The floor is slippery."
No response.
"Alaina, you will slip and fall wearing just your socks!"
Still no response.
CRASH!
"Waaaah! Daddy, I'm hurt!"

Exchanges like this happen almost daily in my house, and they happen almost every second all around the world. Did it hurt me to see my daughter fall? Yes, it did. But if I had run in and put Alaina's shoes on for her, she would have missed two very important lessons: (1) Shoes are for her protection, and (2) Dad knows what he's talking about.

God sets up rules, boundaries, and guidelines. We ignore them and do our own thing. Disaster strikes, and who do we blame? You guessed it—God.

Sometimes the bad things that happen to us are natural consequences of our own behavior. God has chosen not to interfere with our decision making unless we ask for help.

Merciful Father, forgive me when I ignore your laws. I know that I am responsible for my own choices. Help me to know your Word and obey it the best I can. I know your laws and commands are for my benefit. Amen.

 # MARCH 9 MAKING EXCUSES

Happy are those whose transgression is forgiven, whose sin is covered. Happy are those . . . in whose spirit there is no deceit.
—Psalm 32:1-2 (NRSV)

The following are actual statements found on automobile insurance forms submitted by drivers who attempted to summarize the details of an accident in the fewest words possible:

- A pedestrian hit me and went under my car.
- An invisible car came out of nowhere, struck my car, and vanished.
- The indirect cause of the accident was a little guy in a small car with a big mouth.

When something bad happens to us, we sometimes feel the need to assign blame to something or someone else. Even when our own actions have contributed to our predicament, we still try to excuse ourselves from any blame.

It's important to "own" our behavior—to recognize our part in bad decisions or actions. After all, we're not fooling God, are we? Adam, Eve, Cain, and everyone since has tried to hide or make excuses for damaging behavior. But the same God who saw through those situations sees through ours.

Have mercy on me, O God, according to your unfailing love. I am sorry for both the mistakes and the excuses I have made. Give me wisdom and strength not to repeat my mistakes or try to excuse them. Amen.

MARCH 10 "SHARED CONTROL"

But the Spirit produces love, joy, peace, patience, kindness, good-ness, faithfulness, humility and self-control. There is no law against such things as these. And those who belong to Christ Jesus have put to death their human nature with all its passions and desires. The Spirit has given us life; he must also control our lives. —Galatians 5:22-25 (TEV)

If we always would control our desires and think through the long-term outcomes of our decisions, we would avoid many unfortunate situations. When we read God's Word, we discover two strange things about self-control: (1) It doesn't always come from within yourself, and (2) you have to give it up in order to get it.

Even though our sinful nature has corrupted our thoughts and desires, God has provided us a weapon to use in the battle for self-control—the Holy Spirit. In fact, self-control is a "fruit of the Spirit." By giving up control of your spirit to God's Spirit, you have a powerful ally in tempting situations. Self-control actually becomes "shared control" when you allow God to have the steering wheel of your life.

Spirit of God, I give you control today. Help me with my decisions, temptations, and attitudes so that I can bear the fruit of your Holy Spirit—the fruit of self-control. Amen.

MARCH 11 THE HIGH PRICE OF FREE WILL

The Lord does not easily become angry, but he is powerful and never lets the guilty go unpunished. —Nahum 1:3 (TEV)

"I want to believe in God, but because of what my dad did to me . . . it's just real difficult to." —Jessica, age 13

Jessica is not alone. Hundreds of your peers—and perhaps even you— have been the victim of some form of abuse.

If our free will decisions hurt only ourselves, we could understand better why bad things happen. But, unfortunately, our free will decisions to break God's laws can have a serious impact on others. When something bad happens to an innocent person because of another person's decision or action, we are stunned. We don't see God stopping the schoolyard shooter, the drunk driver, the abusive parent. Because the victim played no part in caus-ing the tragedy, it is difficult to deal with. But God does not ignore these situations.

Although God does not prevent bad free will decisions, God does promise punishment and ultimate judgment. The freedom to make choices sometimes carries a high price.

Dear Lord, give me strength to overcome the pain I've received at the hands of others. Let me also be aware of the pain I have caused others, and help me to seek forgiveness. Amen.

GOD IS IN CONTROL

"For I know the plans I have for you," declares the LORD, "plans to prosper you and not to harm you, plans to give you hope and a future."
—Jeremiah 29:11

Sometimes life just doesn't make sense. Senseless tragedies, natural disasters, crippling diseases—the list goes on and on. Why would God allow these things to happen—especially to those who call him Lord?

This is one of the most difficult things to wrap our faith around: Sometimes bad things happen, and we can't always explain why. But we know that God loves us and wants what's best for us; the Bible makes this perfectly clear. And ultimately, God's plan will be accomplished because he is sovereign. Yes, our world is imperfect and often painful. But there's one thing we can be certain of: God is in control, even when it doesn't appear so, even when chaos is raging all around us. No matter how hopeless we may feel, God can restore our hope and give us a future worth living for.

Heavenly Father, I know you are in control. Sometimes I don't see your work, and sometimes I don't understand your plan or your timing. But I want to have a strong faith to see me through the times that don't make sense. Amen.

SEEING THE GOOD IN BAD SITUATIONS

And we know that in all things God works for the good of those who love him, who have been called according to his purpose.
—Romans 8:28

The atheist says that our world was formed from random forces and that random forces continue to work in our world. There is no "good" or "bad." Stuff just happens. Pretty dim view of life, isn't it?

Why, then, can we see good come out of bad circumstances? The truth is, we can point to many situations where something good has come from something bad. That couldn't be true in a universe ruled by chaos.

Ours is not a world of chance. God is in control, working for good *in all things*. God can bring good from even the worst situations in your life. The same God who turned his own Son's death on a cross into victory over sin and death can turn your defeats into victories.

Dear God, please help me to see the good in bad situations. I know it is not your will for your children to suffer needlessly. I trust in your divine plan, hurt and all, and ask for strength to live that plan out in my life. Amen.

MARCH 14 A BALANCE OF FAITH AND REASON

My friends, consider yourselves fortunate when all kinds of trials come your way, for you know that when your faith succeeds in facing such trials, the result is the ability to endure. . . . But when you pray, you must believe and not doubt at all. Whoever doubts is like a wave in the sea that is driven and blown about by the wind. —James 1:2, 3, 6 (TEV)

The world is full of Scullys and Mulders. Anyone who watches "The X-Files" is familiar with this duo of investigators. Dana Scully is a trained scientist and natural skeptic. Fox Mulder is open to the unexplained. He "wants to believe." Throughout the show's episodes, Mulder has been forced to question some of his beliefs, and Scully has witnessed things her science cannot explain. Both Scully and Mulder would be much shallower without the other's influence.

At some point, every one of us has faced or will face difficult circumstances. When hurtful, negative things happen, are you a Scully or a Mulder? Do you need explanations for everything, or are you content to believe that some things remain a mystery? Or do you have a balance of faith and reason?

No matter how much we know, there will always be "the unknown." When bad things happen, we need faith to keep believing that the truth is "out there," and we need reason to help us discern it.

My God, you are both known and unknown. Sometimes you are "hidden," but you always reveal yourself, in both good and bad circumstances. Help me to have a balance of faith and reason in my life. Help me to have faith like a child, without thinking like one. Amen.

WHAT CAN YOU CONTROL?

The waves of death were all around me; the waves of destruction overwhelmed me. The danger of death was around me, and the grave set its trap for me. In my trouble I called to the LORD; I called to my God for help. In his temple he heard my voice; he listened to my cry for help.
—2 Samuel 22:5-7 (TEV)

"We cannot control the wind, but we can adjust the sails."
—motivational poster

When we ride a rollercoaster, part of the "rush" comes from being out of control. We're strapped in, and we can't change our mind once we start climbing that big hill. There is a momentary thrill of the unknown—of giving up control to something dangerous and unfamiliar. Then when the ride's over, we laugh at our fear and regain control. We knew it wouldn't last forever.

But sometimes life's circumstances are anything but thrilling. Sometimes circumstances beyond our control can overwhelm us. They hit us from out of the blue, and we feel helpless and powerless.

We've seen that good can come out of bad situations. Many times the only thing we have control over is our reaction—our attitude. Like rollercoaster rides, painful times will eventually end. God can give us the strength to endure them and go on.

Heavenly Father, sometimes I feel like I'm not in control of anything. Help me to recognize those things over which I do have control—my relationship with you, my attitude, and my decision to have faith that you will bring me through bad times. Amen.

"I JUST DON'T GET IT"

What we see now is like a dim image in a mirror; then we shall see face to face. What I know now is only partial; then it will be complete—as complete as God's knowledge of me.   —1 Corinthians 13:12 (TEV)

"The biggest room in heaven is going to be the 'Museum of Things I Just Don't Get.'"

—radio comedian Tom Griswold

If people from Poland are called "Poles," why aren't people from Holland called "Holes"? If a pig loses its voice, is it disgruntled?

More seriously, how did God get here? Why does God remain invisible? Let's face it, some things we just don't get. We can get caught up in asking questions that no one this side of heaven can know. Because these questions can't be answered, our faith can suffer, and we can begin to doubt everything we cannot prove.

Fortunately, the Word of God tells us that some day, life's mysteries will be explained. The big questions will be answered when we are finally in God's presence. But until then, don't let unanswerable questions be a roadblock to your walk of faith.

> **Creator God, your creation has many mysteries, confusing questions, and puzzling situations. Help me to anchor my faith in the things I know: that you created me, that you love me, and that you want fellowship with me. Amen.**

MARCH 17   GOD LOVES YOU— FOR REAL

Remember that the Lord your God is the only God and that he is faithful. He will keep his covenant and show his constant love to a thousand generations of those who love him and obey his commands.
—*Deuteronomy 7:9 (TEV)*

"God loves you!" We've heard that for a long time. But is it really true? Aren't we talking about an invisible, all-powerful, nothing-like-us, supernatural creative force? If there really is this mysterious being who lives outside of time on another dimension (cue the creepy soundtrack . . .), how can we possibly know this being loves us? And how can we even relate to God, much less love God back?

Genesis starts out with God creating things—stars, the Earth, animals, people. After creating all this out of nothing, God says "Cool!" and promptly leaves to start another project, right? Wrong. A big clue that an all-powerful Creator God could love us is that God didn't leave creation alone. God entered a dialogue with us. Genesis describes God asking Adam and Eve questions, not just thundering out commands. God obviously desires interaction with us. God loves you—for real.

> **God, help me look and listen for the ways you are trying to communicate with me, and help me keep the channels open so that I can hear you—and respond. Amen.**

MARCH 18

YOU ARE
A WORK OF ART

God looked at everything he had made, and he was very pleased.
Evening passed and morning came . . . that was the sixth day.
—*Genesis 1:31 (TEV)*

Some artists and musicians get very defensive when someone calls their work "good" or "bad." "Art and music are above good or bad," they say. "They're neutral; you should just let them be."

Lucky for us, God didn't have that attitude. Another clue that God loves us is that he called creation "good"—not just once, but several times. We never read of God saying, "Hmmm, this has potential" or "Next time I'll try something different." God does not stay neutral on his "art." God called creation good from the start. And notice that after creating people, God proclaimed everything very good.

People are clearly something special. You are a person worthy of your Creator's attention and concern. You are a work of art, and you are "good."

Heavenly Father, you are truly an artist. You made everything, but you didn't stop there. You were pleased with your work, and you were very pleased with your human creations. Thank you for loving me personally. Thank you for creating me as a special, unique work of art. Amen.

MARCH 19

SET APART

So God created human beings, making them to be like himself.
He created them male and female, blessed them, and said,
"Have many children so that your descendants will live all over
the earth and bring it under their control. I am putting you in
charge of the fish, the birds and all the wild animals."* —*Genesis 1:27 (TEV)*

I once heard Robin Williams say on a TV special, "God's got to have a sense of humor . . . look at a platypus!" There certainly are a lot of creatures on the canvas of God's creation. Researchers who venture into the Brazilian rainforest are discovering new species almost weekly. So are we just another animal among the millions of others in a biology text? Some scientists would have us believe so. Have you heard the saying, "You're just a few chromosomes away from being a chimp or a shrimp"?

Evolutionists tell us that we fought our way to the top of the food chain because, by chance, we evolved bigger brains (at least some of us did) and opposable thumbs. But the Bible tells a different story. God put humans in charge of things by design, not by chance. We have a special place in God's natural order.

Creator God, thank you for making me different. Thank you for setting me apart from the animal kingdom and loving me enough to give me a special place in your creation. Amen.

GOD CARES WHEN YOU ARE LONELY

Then the Lord God said, "It is not good for the man to live alone. I will make a suitable companion to help him."
—*Genesis 2:18 (TEV)*

Ever been in a large crowd and felt completely alone? As you looked around at all the people talking and laughing, you wondered how anyone could possibly know what you were going through inside. Sure, we can try to pretend everything is great in our lives, but deep down, we wonder if anyone cares about us at all.

Today's scripture gives us a double-shot of good news. First, God empathizes with loneliness. We know this from reading the scripture. "It is not good for the man to live alone," God said. But the Creator did not stop there. God then took action and created woman. A careless, unconcerned creator might have said, "Well, here's the earth and all its animals. Good luck, Adam!" This was not the case. God knew Adam would be lonely even before Adam did. And God knows when you are lonely, too.

My God and my Creator, thank you for never leaving me when I feel lonely. I know you love me enough to do something about my loneliness. Amen.

GOD'S LOVE IS EXTREME

This is how we know what love is: Christ gave his life for us. We too, then, ought to give our lives for [others]!
—*1 John 3:16 (TEV)*

Man, did we ever blow it! We had it all—fresh food, clean water, great weather, no disease, and daily talks with the supreme Creator of the universe. We didn't even have to spend money on clothes. But that one act of disobedience destroyed our perfect relationship. Now, covering our bodies is the least of our worries (you could say Adam put the fig in Hilfiger).

How could God ever love such a rebellious and selfish creation? Didn't we get what we deserved? True, there were some heavy consequences for sin, but God never gave up on us. We see God trying to "get back together" with us throughout history. Even though our Creator had every reason to abandon us, he never did. In fact, God went to a terrible extreme to demonstrate this love for you.

Dear Lord God, I am so grateful you did not give up on your creation. Thank you for loving me first, and for showing that love so many times when I've failed. Amen.

MARCH 22 "WHAT HAS GOD EVER DONE FOR ME?"

When we are punished, it seems to us at the time something to make us sad, not glad. Later, however, those who have been disciplined by such punishment reap the peaceful reward of a righteous life. —Hebrews 12:11 (TEV)

"What has God ever done for me?" asked the fourteen-year-old I was counseling. "He didn't keep me from getting into trouble. He didn't help me get out of jail. . . . God never gave me nothing I asked for."

Jeremy had the notion that God was a celestial vending machine—that God was supposed to prevent him from making bad choices or protect him from the consequences of those choices. We talked some more and discovered something: A good father may not give a child everything he or she *wants*, but he will give the child everything he or she *needs*. We also agreed that God did give us something—something very precious.

When God came to earth in human form, it was for our benefit. We needed Jesus to conquer sin and death. We sure couldn't do it on our own! Jesus gave up everything when he took on our mortality. How great God's love for us must be!

Heavenly Father, I know you love me. I know this because of Jesus' sacrifice on my behalf. I'm sorry I don't recognize the gifts you give me sometimes. I am grateful for all you have done for me. Amen.

MARCH 23 GOD'S GREATEST GIFT

He always had the nature of God, but he did not think that by force he should try to remain equal to God. Instead of this, of his own free will he gave up all he had and took on the nature of a servant. He became like a [human being] and appeared in human likeness.

—*Philippians 2:6, 7 (TEV)*

Have you ever received a thoughtless gift? Something that looks like the person picked it up at the discount store on the way to your party? You can usually tell if the gift-giver has invested in the present. How the gift is wrapped, whether it's something you really need or want, how much of a sacrifice it took to give it—these are all factors that can tell us how much the gift-giver cares for us.

These same "clues" also give us some insight into how much God cares for us. As our "gift," Jesus was made vulnerable to all the frailties of mortal life—sickness, pain, hunger, and so forth. God took the chance that some would return his gift unopened, but still he gave it. Jesus' sacrifice was "just what we needed" to conquer death and reconcile us with our Creator. You can know that God loves you because he invested heavily in his gift.

Lord God, thank you for the gift of your Son, Jesus, on my behalf. I know you care for me because you made such a sacrifice for me. Help me show my thanks to you by daily growing closer to you. Amen.

MARCH 24

AN INCREDIBLE SACRIFICE

But God has shown us how much he loves us—it was while we were still sinners that Christ died for us! —*Romans 5:8 (TEV)*

Let's say you've never made more than a 2.0 grade point average. As you enter your senior year, your parents make a deal with you: Maintain a 3.5 GPA your senior year, and you'll get a new car on graduation day. You study and struggle, but at midterm you still have only a 2.8. Now imagine coming home and seeing a brand new car in your driveway. Your parents have sold one of their cars to buy it for you "just in case you make your grades." Incredible parents, right?

Well, that's just what God did for us. Jesus died for us while we were still in sin. He didn't wait until we "pulled our grades up." (Under our own power, we never could anyway!) God even knew that many of his children would never accept his gift. What incredible love God must have to make such a sacrifice "just in case"!

Dear Jesus, how incredible that you died for me before I "made the grade." I know that without your sacrifice, I would have failed for sure. Amen.

JESUS "TOOK THE HEAT" FOR YOU

Everyone must die once, and after that be judged by God. In the same manner, Christ also was offered in sacrifice once to take away the sins of many. He will appear a second time, not to deal with sin, but to save those who are waiting for him. —Hebrews 9:27 (TEV)

When we don't get what we deserve, that's a real good thing.
—from "Real Good Thing,"
The Newsboys (Words and music by
Jody Davis, Peter Furler, and Steve Taylor)

Grace involves getting something good that we don't deserve. It also involves not getting something bad that we *do* deserve! For the selfishness, disobedience, and rebellious nature of the human race, God had every right to destroy his creations as he did during Noah's day. Instead of saving a few and sacrificing millions, though, God chose to save millions by the sacrifice of one man.

You can have faith that God loves you because he chose to spare you. In fact, God chose to spare *all* of us from the wrath we deserve. Jesus took the heat for everyone's sin so that we might be in fellowship with God again. Jesus taught that there's no greater love than laying down your life for a friend. Then he demonstrated it by dying in our place.

Heavenly Father, I am so grateful for the sacrifice your Son made on my behalf. Sometimes I still want to run from you or do my own thing. When that happens, I ask you to remind me of how I was spared your wrath by Jesus' sacrifice. Amen.

A BALANCED VIEW OF GOD

We were God's enemies, but he has made us his friends through the death of his Son. Now that we are God's friends, how much more will we be saved by Christ's life! —Romans 5:10 (TEV)

Blaise Pascal wrote that believing in God without acknowledging our wretchedness—our sinfulness—leads to pride. On the other hand, acknowledging our sinfulness without believing in God leads to despair. Only Christ can give us the right balance, he said, because Christ helps us to know both God and our sinfulness.

Pascal lived in the 1620s, but he's still right on the money. We can still get into trouble by focusing on either extreme. Many in our generation live a lifestyle of despair. Let's face it, this generation has seen a lot of wretchedness.

In the same way, we can have a skewed view of God. We can see God's loving side—God's efforts to bring us back into fellowship, his provision for us—and start thinking God's just a softie who would never punish anyone. Jesus gave the world a reality check. He pointed out both our wretchedness and our value in God's eyes. In the same way, he also gave us a balanced view of God's character.

Creator God, help me to see both sides of myself, and to see both sides of you. I don't want to fall into despair or pride. Amen.

MARCH 27 JESUS SHOWED US WHAT GOD IS LIKE

Jesus answered, "For a long time I have been with you all; yet you do not know me, Philip? Whoever has seen me has seen the Father." —John 14:9 (TEV)

"Jesus was a vegetarian."
—controversial California billboard

Many people have made some "creative" claims about God and Jesus. Whenever you hear someone say, "God is like this" or "God thinks this," a red flag should pop up in your mind. How can this person know what God is like? For that matter, how can *any* of us begin to know what God is like?

Only one person has made a convincing case for knowing the mind of God: Jesus Christ himself. Jesus spoke with authority. He knew what he was talking about. How did he know? Jesus said, "I and the Father are one" (John 10:30). If that is true (and there's much evidence in the Bible to support his claim), then Jesus' characterizations of God are totally trustworthy. We can have faith that God loves us because Jesus revealed to us God's nature and "person-ality."

If you want to catch a glimpse of God and his incredible love for you, look to Jesus!

Lord Jesus, I believe that you and the Father are one. Through your insights into God's character, let me know I am loved. Help me to understand what my Creator is like, and what he thinks of me. Amen.

MARCH 28

IMITATING CHRIST

Imitate me, then, just as I imitate Christ.
—1 Corinthians 11:1 (TEV)

I once heard of a guy who was stopped for not wearing his seatbelt—and the policeman who gave him the ticket was on a motorcycle! Apparently, the officer failed to appreciate the irony of the situation. "I suppose," said the man, "If I'd been on top of my vehicle, like the cop, it would have been O.K."

Unfortunately, "Do what I say, not what I do" has been modeled by many people in authority. People lose credibility and respect when their behavior flies in the face of the rules they supposedly enforce. Jesus didn't fall into that trap. The example he set was a perfect blueprint of God's nature. Jesus was without sin, loved unconditionally, and forgave those who were willing to change. By looking at what Jesus did and what he said about God and God's kingdom, we get a more complete picture of God. We also get a picture of the kind of people God wants us to become.

Dear Lord, help me when I study your ways and your words. I want to know God more completely. Holy Spirit, show me God's love, God's nature, and God's character as I study the example of Jesus Christ. And help me to imitate those qualities and characteristics. Amen.

MARCH 29

YOU MATTER TO GOD

For only a penny you can buy two sparrows, yet not one sparrow falls to the ground without your Father's consent. As for you, even the hairs of your head have all been counted. So do not be afraid; you are worth much more than many sparrows! —*Matthew 10:29 (TEV)*

"Billions of solar systems forming a galaxy," says the science guy on TV, "billions of galaxies scattered across infinite space. And what lies beyond? No one knows for sure."

Learning about our universe can leave us feeling pretty insignificant. Earth can seem like a grain of sand at the bottom of the ocean, and Earth's inhabitants—that's us—seem even less important. Even we who believe in a Creator feel alone sometimes. With all that space out there, why would God pay attention to our little corner of the universe?

According to Jesus, our Creator is even more observant than that. Not only does the Father care about people, he notices when a single sparrow falls from a tree—now that's attention to detail! Jesus characterized God as a compassionate creator who loves his creation. We may be small by comparison, but not small enough to escape God's eye.

Heavenly Father, sometimes I feel so insignificant. In a busy and confusing world, help me to feel your love for me—and to know that I matter to you. Amen.

MARCH 30 — YOU CAN RUN, BUT YOU CAN'T HIDE

Or suppose a woman who has ten silver coins loses one of them—what does she do? She lights a lamp, sweeps her house, and looks carefully everywhere until she finds it. When she finds it, she calls her friends and neighbors together and says to them, "I am so happy I found the coin I lost. Let us celebrate!" In the same way, I tell you the angels of God rejoice over one sinner who repents. —Luke 15:8-10 (TEV)

In the movie *The Fugitive*, there is a huge, coordinated effort to find one man. Tommy Lee Jones' character is relentless in pursuing Harrison Ford. He is willing to cross any terrain and risk any injury to bring back his man. There's no way a U.S. Marshall would mount such a huge search and rescue effort without a burning desire to see a fugitive brought to justice.

When Jesus told the parables of the lost sheep, lost coin, and prodigal son, he painted a similar picture of God's mission: to bring us back into fellowship with him. God's motivation is love. No matter how we try to run from God— and even if we don't know we're running—God is in pursuit. The hounds of heaven are on our trail. There's no way God would mount such a huge "search and rescue" effort if he didn't love us and desire a relationship with us.

Father, God, forgive me for the times I've run from you. Thank you for your persistence in tracking me down. I know I can't hide from your loving pursuit. Help me not to stray from you and your will for me. Amen.

MARCH 31 — GOD IS NEVER FAR AWAY

Who will separate us from the love of Christ? Will hardship, or distress, or persecution, or famine, or nakedness, or peril, or sword? As it is written, "For your sake we are being killed all day long; we are accounted as sheep to be slaughtered." No, in all these things we are more than conquerors through him who loved us. —Romans 8:35-37 (NRSV)

This month we've considered "why bad things happen." We've seen that we live in a fallen world—a world where we're free to make bad choices; a world where things happen that we don't understand. We've also considered how much God loves and cares for us. We've wrestled with "good and evil" and discovered that we weren't created to fully understand either one.

When bad things happen, don't let yourself fall into the trap of blaming God. Instead, ask yourself: (1) Was this situation the result of someone's free-will choice (e.g., violence, rebellion)? (2) Was it a result of "original sin" (e.g., sickness, disease)? or (3) Was it a random tragedy with no apparent meaning (e.g., tornado, car accident)?

During or after a painful situation, we look for answers, justice, or some kind of resolution. Answers may seem far away. Justice may seem far away. Resolution may seem far away. But God is never far away. We cannot be separated from God's love; we only can be distracted from seeing it.

Merciful God, I know you are big enough to handle my questions and my doubts. Through all my confusion and questioning, let my faith be increased. I want to come out on the other side of difficult situations, look back, and see your hand at work. Amen.

APRIL

AS I LAY ME DOWN TO SLEEP

Anne Marie Drew

APRIL

AS I LAY ME DOWN TO SLEEP

Anne Marie Drew

APRIL 1

CHERISHED BY GOD

The LORD is my shepherd, I shall not want.
—Psalm 23:1 (NSRV)

My favorite lullaby is "Tender Shepherd" from the original *Peter Pan* movie. The gentle song coaxes many infants—and even grownups—to sleep by reminding them that there is a tender shepherd who lovingly watches over us at day's end. Once we are no longer small children, we sometimes need more than lullabies to fall asleep peacefully. Feelings of awkwardness and anger and not belonging can ruin any chance of sweet dreams. Though these meditations are not lullabies, read them at night if you can. Let them remind you how precious and irreplaceable you are and how infinitely cherished by God. Let them remind you about all the hopeful possibilities that are before you and next to you. No matter how troubled the day has been, no matter how worried or hurt you may be, imagine yourself nestled softly asleep in the presence of a God who will never abandon you—a God who surrounds you with much goodness.

Tender Shepherd, let me feel your love. Amen.

APRIL 2

KINDERGARTEN MEMORIES

And remember, I am with you always.
—Matthew 28:20 (NRSV)

Picture your kindergarten classroom. Take your time, and don't worry if, at first, you can't seem to remember too many details.

What did the bulletin boards look like? Where did you sit in relation to the teacher's desk? Was there a piano? Were there windows? Were there plants? Toys? Close your eyes and try to picture yourself inside your small body, sitting at your desk or table. What does it feel like to be so small?

Try to remember the feel of your chair, the texture of crayons, the coolness of a blank sheet of drawing paper.

Now imagine that Jesus Christ is sitting in the chair next to you, watching you. And at the end of a school day, he wants to tell you something. He has watched as you drew a picture and ate a snack and sang a song and smiled at your teacher. He has been right there sitting in the chair next to you, loving you.

As he scoops you up in his arms at the end of the day, what does he say to you?

Lord, as I sleep, keep me surrounded by your love. Amen.

APRIL 3

YOU ARE A BLESSING

If I love you more, will you love me less?
—*2 Corinthians 12:15b (NIV)*

Think about your favorite relative—someone whose face lights up when you walk in the door. Maybe it's your grandmother or grandfather. Maybe you have a favorite aunt or uncle. Or perhaps there is someone with whom you just "click"—a person whose company you enjoy, a person with whom you seldom fight or disagree, a person who thinks of you as a special blessing.

Call to mind a day that you spent with this special relative or friend. Try to remember a specific day, and let your memory fill in the details. In your mind's eye, watch yourself closely as you spend time with this person. How do you spend the day? What do you talk about? Do you run errands together? Watch a favorite TV program?

As you fall asleep tonight, think about how your very existence makes this special person happy.

Lord Jesus, help me to remember that I am a blessing. Amen.

CHILDHOOD GIFTS

Thanks be to God for his indescribable gift!
—2 Corinthians 9:15 (NRSV)

Can you remember the little gifts you made as a child for your friends and relatives?

There were marigolds planted in Styrofoam cups, necklaces made out of macaroni, hand prints molded in plaster, and ornaments made from cookie dough.

Can you remember watching as someone hung your handmade ornament on the Christmas tree? Can you still see a picture you brought home proudly displayed on the refrigerator? Can you recall the look on someone's face when you presented one of your special treasures?

Take some time to remember the gifts you made when you were a child. Think about how much love you poured into those creations. Since you were very small, you have been making people happy.

Lord, fill my dreams with images of the gifts I have given to those I love. Amen.

WHILE YOU SLEEP

And Jesus said to him, "Foxes have holes, and birds of the air have nests; but the Son of Man has nowhere to lay his head."
—Luke 9:58 (NRSV)

Jesus Christ didn't complain much, but he must have regretted not having a regular bed those three years of his public ministry. Even the sparrows and cardinals and orioles have places to sleep, he suggested, but the Son of Man had nowhere to lay his head. Imagining Jesus Christ sleeping in a bed is tricky. Even harder is imagining Jesus being tucked under the covers by someone who loved him. He was always on the move.

When we fall asleep at night, however, we do have a place to lay our heads. Maybe the bed is a mess, loaded with cookie crumbs and CDs and dirty socks, but we can burrow down under the covers and feel safe and surrounded by comfortable blankets. As you drift to sleep, think of your bed as the palm of God's hand. Then, nestled safely and softly in that hand, remember that God watches you while you sleep.

Thank you, Lord, for giving me a place to rest my head. Amen.

SMALL ACTS OF KINDNESS

Then he will answer them, "Truly I tell you, just as you did not do it to one of the least of these, you did not do it to me."
—*Matthew 25:45 (NRSV)*

Think about all the good things you did today for other people.

You did more good than you can remember. You probably smiled at dozens of people. Even if you were in a grumpy mood, you probably lent someone a pencil or held open a door. Maybe you helped make dinner or cleared the table. Did you say hello to your neighbor? Did you listen to a friend's troubles? Walk the dog? Feed the cat?

Sometimes the little things we do matter so much more than the big accomplishments. The small, unremembered acts of kindness that you perform can transform your little part of God's kingdom.

Lord, as I fall asleep, help me to remember one of my good deeds that I may have forgotten. Amen.

THE QUIET SOUNDS OF NIGHT

"Be still, and know that I am God!"   —*Psalm 46:10 (NRSV)*

Have you ever seen reruns of the old TV series "The Waltons"? At the end of each show, we hear the family calling out "Good Night" to each other. As the camera pulls away and we see the old farmhouse, we watch as the lights go out in each bedroom. The home seems serene and peaceful and filled with love.

No matter where we live or with whom, at night when our own homes are quiet and all the activity of the day is done, we can sometimes hear sounds we miss during the day. Can you hear the wind chimes on the porch? Or the ticking of a clock? Is a ceiling fan whirring somewhere? The quiet, rhythmic sounds of a home are soothing signs of God's love. Sometimes during the day a home can be filled with too much anger or too much activity; but at night when finally everyone is at rest, the quiet sounds of God's good creation seep through.

Lord Jesus, fill my sleeping home with your presence. Amen.

APRIL 8 · ALL SHALL BE WELL

So do not be afraid; you are of more value than many sparrows.
—Matthew 10:31 (NRSV)

There was a very holy woman named Julian of Norwich, who lived in England in the 1300s. She had a very close relationship with Jesus Christ. Sometimes when she was praying, she'd get very clear images of people suffering and crying. The images saddened and frightened her. During her prayers, she asked God why there had to be so much terrible pain and suffering in the world. God didn't dodge her tough question. The Creator told Julian that evil has to exist, but "All shall be well."

Those four words—all shall be well—are God's assurance that no matter how horrible things may seem on certain days, everything is going to be all right. We don't have to be afraid. Things may seem to be a total mess, but the bad times will pass. And God's love will see us through.

Jesus, please give me a real sense of your peace tonight. Amen.

APRIL 9 · MISTAKES

For you, O Lord, are good and forgiving, abounding in steadfast love.
—Psalm 86:5 (NRSV)

We've all done stuff we're ashamed of. Said nasty things. Hurt people's feelings. Maybe even taken something that didn't belong to us. Sometimes even our best friends don't know about the crummy things we've done.

But God knows and still loves us beyond anything.

Let yourself remember a not-so-good thing you've done, and imagine Jesus Christ looking at you with eyes of compassion and love. As he stands there watching you goof, try to see his face—a face filled with understanding and love for you, even when you slip up.

Making a mistake does not make you a bad person. No matter how serious the error, you belong to God, who loves you.

Lord, remind me that nothing can separate me from you. Amen.

APRIL 10   LOVE YOURSELF

You shall love your neighbor as yourself.   —Mark 12:31 (NRSV)

Were you kind to yourself today? Did you do anything that made yourself feel better?

Did you take time alone? Or spend extra time with your best buddy? Did you eat a favorite food or watch a favorite TV program? Did you listen to some favorite music?

Being good to yourself is very important. When God tells us to love our neighbor as ourselves, our Creator is telling us how important it is to take care of ourselves.

Think about a good thing you did just for yourself today. Remind yourself that God wants you to take care of you—to love yourself. And if you didn't take such good care of yourself today, try being kinder to yourself tomorrow.

Lord, help me to be kind to myself. Amen.

APRIL 11   CAN'T SLEEP?

And a voice came from heaven, "You are my Son, the Beloved; with you I am well pleased."   —Luke 3:22 (NRSV)

If you were baptized as a baby, you may not remember anything at all about the event. If you were older when you were baptized, your memories might be clearer. If you have not yet been baptized, you still have this grace-filled event to look forward to.

God's words at Jesus' baptism are also meant for you. You are God's beloved. God is pleased with you.

Try this little exercise. Repeat the above verse, substituting your name for the word "Son." For example, "You are my Joseph, the beloved; with you I am well pleased." Or "You are my Jennifer, the beloved; with you I am well pleased."

Instead of counting sheep tonight, repeat God's statement of love for you. Repeat the words over and over as you fall asleep.

Lord Jesus, keep reminding me of your love. Amen.

APRIL 12

CAPABLE
OF GREAT LOVE

Follow the way of love and eagerly desire spiritual gifts.
—1 Corinthians 14:1

Look at 1 Corinthians 13:4-7. You probably recognize this passage. We hear these words at many weddings. The apostle Paul is pretty clear about what love is.

Now reread the passage out loud, substituting your name for the word *love*. Every time Paul uses the word *love*, say your name instead. Be sure to read out loud so that you can hear your name.

See how wonderful you sound? You can continually be that person Paul describes. All you have to do is follow the advice he gives at the beginning of the very next chapter: Seek eagerly after love. Set your hearts on spiritual gifts.

Lord, thank you for making me capable of great love. Amen.

APRIL 13

ALL GOD
WANTS YOU TO BE

There is no fear in love, but perfect love casts out fear.
—1 John 4:18 (NRSV)

There's an old story about a boy who thought he was very ugly. This boy fell in love with a girl he thought was beautiful. Afraid that she'd have nothing to do with him, the boy had an artist design a special, very handsome mask. Wearing the handsome mask, the boy introduced himself to the beautiful girl. They dated and fell in love, and he finally asked her to marry him. But before she could say yes, the boy said, "I have to show you something—so that you know the real me." With that, he took off the mask, expecting her to be repulsed by his face. Instead, the young woman said, "Yes? What is it you wanted to show me?" You see, his face had become handsome. He had become the very thing he pretended to be.

If you act brave, you will become brave. If you act kind, you will become kind. If you act courageous, you will become courageous. No one is perfect all at once. But you can become all God wants you to be.

Lord, thank you for making me capable of perfect love. Amen.

APRIL 14
A FUTURE WITH HOPE

For surely I know the plans I have for you, says the LORD, plans for your welfare and not for harm, to give you a future with hope.
—Jeremiah 29:11-12 (NRSV)

Shakespeare's character Macbeth, whom you may know from having read the play by the same name, commits several vicious murders. When he thinks about repenting, he decides he has done so many bad things that there's no hope of turning around and making things better. So, he keeps right on butchering people until he is killed.

Macbeth's thinking could not be more wrong. There is always hope—always a new chance. In many ways, God doesn't care what you did ten minutes ago. God cares what you are doing at this very moment. If today you were in a bad mood and yelled at your brother and were disrespectful to your mom, those aren't good things—but you can always start again tomorrow. God will never turn away from you. Never.

God stands with open arms.

Lord, keep my face turned toward my future of hope. Amen.

APRIL 15
TRADING HEARTS WITH JESUS

"Do not let your hearts be troubled."   *—John 14:1(NSRV)*

Some days are going to be bad ones. Some days you can't "Just Do It" as the Nike ads suggest. You will be grumpy or feel sick or just not be at your best.

But there's a trick that works. Trade hearts with Jesus. The idea is not as silly as it might sound. Just close your eyes and ask Jesus to trade hearts with you for one day. Tell him that you are feeling a little wobbly and that you'd like him to take your shabby heart for one day while you borrow his.

When you fall asleep tonight, know that if tomorrow turns into a rough one, you can let Jesus have your heart for a while—and you'll be fine.

Lord, please give me a heart as strong as yours. Amen.

APRIL 16 — SEEING OTHERS THROUGH GOD'S EYES

They said to him, "Lord, let our eyes be opened."
—Matthew 20:33 (NRSV)

Gloria, one of my students, irritated me every day when she bounced into my classroom. She'd dump her leftover orange peels in my wastepaper basket, making the whole room smell. She'd sing some stupid, loud song, and she'd gab with her friends right until the bell rang—and only then would she make a made dash for her seat.

I couldn't find one good thing about her.

One night I asked God for a favor. "Please, God, let me see Gloria as you see her. How does she look to you?"

And God showed me an outgoing and full-of-life young woman with energy enough to change the world and do great things.

Ever since that night, whenever I've had trouble with a person during the day, I always pray—right before going to bed—to see the person through God's eyes.

God, help me to see everyone I meet through your eyes. Amen.

APRIL 17 — "FLOATING" ON GOD'S LOVE

On that day living waters shall flow out from Jerusalem . . . it
shall continue in summer as in winter.
—Zechariah 14:8 (NRSV)

I earned a D in swimming once because I couldn't float. The funny thing is I really like to float, but I could never quite get the form right. My swimming instructors got frustrated with me.

Although I did not like getting a D, I still like to float, especially in an outdoor pool or lake. The sensation of the water buoying me up and the way all the sounds are muffled—I feel as if I'm surrounded by a huge, watery pillow. I like looking up at the sky as I move along in the water.

Sometimes I think of God's love like that—holding me up, holding up the people I love. Easy and soft, with no rough edges.

Lord of Life, let me sleep in easy softness, with no rough edges. Amen.

APRIL 18

FEELINGS AND FAITH

For David says concerning him, "I saw the Lord always before me, for he is at my right hand so that I will not be shaken."
—*Acts 2:25 (NRSV)*

Watching the two sisters fight in the church pew in front of me was pretty embarrassing.

"Mom," the older one hissed under her breath, "tell Betsy to stop bugging me."

Just as the mom turned to quiet the girls, Betsy grabbed at her sister's arm and dug her nails in hard. The older sister stared in anger at the nail marks in her skin.

Clearly, these girls were not in a mood for church. After their mom shot them an angry glare, they sat in stony silence for the rest of the service. Despite it all, their presence in church was still a good thing.

We sometimes think that if we don't feel a certain way, then we can't really have faith. But real faith has almost nothing to do with feelings. You can be angry or sad or happy or mean and still have great faith. Feelings come and go. At the end of a particularly bad day, you might be tempted to think that because you were in a foul mood all day or because you fought with someone, God was absent from your life.

God is always present, always loving you. You may not always feel God's love. You may not always feel like a person of faith. But you are.

Lord, thank you for standing with me even when I cannot feel you. Amen.

APRIL 19

HOLD ON TO HOPE

"He is not here; for he has been raised, as he said. Come, see the place where he lay."   —*Matthew 28:6 (NRSV)*

In five minutes worth of world news, you can see people starving, babies bombed out of their homes, and high school students running for cover as their classmates open fire. Even if you don't watch the news, you know people, maybe even in your own family, who are suffering terribly from disease or divorce or money troubles or something else.

There is evil all around us. There is a dark side to human existence. But as Christians, we know that evil will never win in the end. Evil did the worst it could do on Good Friday. Evil killed absolute goodness in the person of Jesus Christ. Yet goodness triumphed on Easter Sunday when the

Lord of Life burst forth from the tomb.

Evil will always exist, but we have to remind ourselves to hold on until Easter.

Lord of the empty tomb, thank you for the gift of hope. Amen.

WORK, A GOOD THING?

The LORD God took the man and put him in the garden of Eden to till it and keep it.   —*Genesis 2:15 (NRSV)*

"I'm not mowing the lawn!" Joe screamed at his mother. "You can't make me! Most parents pay their kids to work. You don't pay me anything." His face was twisted and angry as he stomped out of the back door.

Sometimes work seems like a punishment—an unfair task that someone else makes us do. There are so many other things we'd like to be doing. But God never intended work as a punishment. Adam and Eve were working in the Garden of Eden, the most perfect place on earth, *before* they gave in to temptation. God didn't see work as a punishment; he saw it as a good thing.

At the end of a day, it's sometimes good to remember that work is not a curse but a blessing.

Lord, thank you for the gift of work. Amen.

HOW WELL DOES GOD KNOW YOU?

He calls his own sheep by name and leads them out.
                                   —*John 10:3 (NRSV)*

Jesus talks so often about sheep and shepherds that we are tempted to stop paying attention after a while. We think of sheep as big, fluffy balls of fur. Unless we're farmers, most of us never get near the animals.

But in Jesus' time, shepherds really did know each of their sheep. The shepherds fell asleep right at the entrance of the sheephold so that the sheep could not go in or out without their knowledge. At night and again in the morning, the shepherds ran their hands over each individual sheep to make sure there were no cuts or bruises or wounds on the animal.

That's how well God knows us. We can sleep secure in the knowledge that God runs his hands over us and knows all of our wounds and bruises.

Lord, please watch over me. Amen.

BE A GOOD LISTENER

A certain woman named Lydia, a worshiper of God, was listening to us.
—Acts 16:14 (NRSV)

Do you know anyone named Lydia? Is she a good listener? The Lydia of the New Testament was a great listener. And because she listened to the apostle Paul talk about Jesus, she brought her whole household to God.

Listening can seem like a waste of time. We don't like being quiet and sitting still. Talking can be much more fun than listening.

But do you know what it feels like to have someone listen to you, *really* listen? Suddenly you feel as if you are the most important person in the whole world. Listening is a special gift, and we are lucky to be surrounded by people who take the time to hear us.

Tomorrow, try to be a person who listens, and thank God when someone listens to you.

Lord, tomorrow, let me be like Lydia. Amen.

START WHERE YOU ARE

As he was getting into the boat, the man who had been possessed by demons begged him that he might be with him. But Jesus refused, and said to him, "Go home to your friends."
—Mark 5:18-19 (NRSV)

Mother Teresa, the great missionary who took care of the poor, liked to mention a simple fact. Jesus did not say, "Love the whole world." He said, "Love one another." Mother Teresa insisted that by doing little things with great love we can become like Christ. She insisted that washing dishes and peeling potatoes are acts of love. Certainly, going on mission trips to help poor people is important. And our churches will always have programs that need our help. But we have to take care of those closest to us first.

The fellow in this reading from Mark wants to run and tell the whole world that Jesus has healed him. But the Lord turns him around and says, "Go home."

Doing great things starts where we are.

Lord, help me pay attention to the people who are closest to me. Amen.

APRIL 24 — RECOGNIZING JESUS

Guided by the Spirit, Simeon came into the temple; and when the parents brought in the child Jesus, to do for him what was customary under the law, Simeon took him in his arms and praised God. —Luke 2:27-28 (NRSV)

If Jesus Christ walked in at dinner time, sat down in an empty chair at your table, and starting eating spaghetti and meatballs with your family, would you recognize him? How about if he showed up at your next baseball game or soccer match? Or what if he came through the drive-thru at McDonald's while you were working at the window? He might be tough to spot, especially if he were dressed in modern clothes.

Simeon recognized Jesus when he was a baby in the temple because he'd been praying for so long that he recognized God. He'd been waiting for this moment for his whole life. He knew what was expected of him.

If we quietly pay attention to God at the end of every day, we won't be surprised whenever and wherever he shows up—even at the drive-thru window.

Lord, help me to recognize you in my life. Amen.

APRIL 25 — WHEN YOU'RE HURTING

And wherever he went, into villages or cities or farms, they laid the sick in the marketplaces, and begged him that they might touch even the fringe of his cloak; and all who touched it were healed. —Mark 6:56 (NRSV)

In the movie *The Hiding Place*, we see Corrie ten Boom and her sister treated like animals while in a Nazi concentration camp during World War II. The movie, in places, is too horrible to watch. But the sisters learn a powerful lesson about God: "There is no well so deep that He is not deeper still." We can stand before the powers of hell, and God will be right next to us.

Our hurts may never be as severe as those of Corrie ten Boom and her sister, but the cruel remarks of others will still hurt us. When our parents get angry at us, we'll still feel miserable. If a boyfriend or girlfriend dumps us for someone else, we are going to feel sick. The pain may not go away immediately; but little by little, if we talk over our emotional and physical pain with Jesus Christ, he will make things better.

Mark is so clear when he says, "All who touched him got well."

Lord, the next time I'm hurting, remind me to reach out to you. Amen.

APRIL 26 — A SURE SIGN

Let anyone with ears to hear listen! —Mark 4:9 (NRSV)

Jesus Christ may be a nice and kind shepherd, but he's also a very strict taskmaster, too. We sometimes goof by making him into a soft and gooey person. There's a song called "Glory" in the musical *Pippin,* and there's a line in the song that says, "War is strict as Jesus."

Jesus is strict. He doesn't let us get away with being our worst selves. He wants us to be perfect. In the fourth chapter of Mark, from which today's verse is taken, it's easy to see how stern Jesus can be when people fall away from the right path. He will keep nudging us and nudging us until we are reminded that everything we are must be turned back to him. And that nudging is a sure sign of his love for us.

Lord, thank you for loving me enough to nudge me back to you. Amen.

APRIL 27 — ALWAYS ON THE MOVE

And immediately he got into the boat with his disciples and went to the district of Dalmanutha. —Mark 8:10 (NRSV)

See if you can find a map of the Holy Land. Any simple one will do. Your Bible might even have one.

Then read this passage from Mark and look at how many miles Jesus walked throughout his ministry. Look at the size of the territory he covered on foot. After performing the miracle of the loaves and the fishes, for example, he set off for the neighborhood of Dalmanutha, a town on the west coast of the Sea of Galilee. He was always on the move.

Our relationship with Jesus has many dimensions. One dimension is understanding him as a human being in a given historical and geographical space. It can be exciting, really, to "walk" with Jesus across the rugged hills of the Holy Land.

Remember, he was always on the move to spread his message of love.

Lord, keep traveling to find me so that I never stray from your circle of love. Amen.

CHOOSE WHAT IS GOOD

Don't let evil get the upper hand but conquer evil by doing good.
—Romans 12:21 (TLB)

"Everyone at the lunch table is so glad you finally stopped eating with us. No one really likes you."

I still remember how horrible I felt, in the eighth grade, when a girl said these cruel words to me. New to the school, I had sat at lunch table after lunch table, trying to find a group of friends to eat with. No one wanted me around. One day, when I had given up on yet another table and was eating by myself in the cafeteria, a girl came over and made the dreadful remark as she emptied her lunch tray into the trash. I went home sobbing.

My Dad came to the rescue. "Honey," he said, when I wouldn't stop feeling sorry for myself, "you can't control what will happen to you in life. You can control how you react to it."

He was right. We always have a choice to focus on what is bad or what is good. By choosing not only to focus on what is good but also to *do* what is good—even when others are cruel and hurtful to us—we can conquer evil.

Dear Lord, help me choose to focus on what is good and then to do good. Amen.

PATIENCE REQUIRED

But as for that in the good soil, these are the ones who, when they hear the word, hold it fast in an honest and good heart, and bear fruit with patient endurance. *—Luke 8:15 (NRSV)*

You may have seen this popular saying on a poster, bumper sticker, or T-shirt: *Please be patient with me. God's not finished with me yet.*

How true these words are. Sometimes non-Christians look at us and call us hypocrites because we commit sins and do not always act Christ-like. Because we do not behave perfectly, they think that we are not really who we say we are—that we are not followers of Jesus Christ; that we are just fakes.

Yet Jesus knows that we are limited by our very humanity, just as his disciples were. When the disciples failed to understand the miracle of the loaves and the fishes, for example, Jesus said to them, "Do you have eyes but fail to see, and ears but fail to hear?" (Mark 8:18). So often, Jesus felt let down and disappointed by his disciples. But he patiently waited for them to understand.

Patience is required.

Lord, teach me to be patient with myself as I try to become more like you. Amen.

APRIL 30 — HAPPY MEMORIES

You shall be happy, and it shall go well with you.
—Psalm 128:2 (NRSV)

What was your happiest day ever? Is there one tucked inside your memory? Can you pull it out and look at it as you fall asleep? Were there people with you? Or maybe you were alone? Can you relive the day in your mind's eye?

God gave you that day and the memory of that day—the memory to remind you that you are well loved and surrounded by goodness all the days of your life.

Fall asleep remembering the happiest day. And remember that there are more to come.

You are greatly loved.

Lord, thank you for happy memories. Amen.

--Anne Marie Drew

MAY

SO MANY QUESTIONS

Harriette Cross

SO MANY QUESTIONS

Harriette Cross

WHO AM I?

For you created my inmost being; you knit me together in my mother's womb. I praise you because I am fearfully and wonderfully made; your works are wonderful, I know that full well.
—Psalm 139:13-14

As we grow up, there comes a time when we ask "Who am I?" and "Where do I fit into this huge world?" We wonder what God had in mind when we were created. The more we ask questions, the less others seem to have the answers.

Psalm 139 can be a comfort to us because it tells us that even before we ask the questions, God already has the answers. Before we were born, God had a plan for our lives. God knows our questions, our hopes, our thoughts, and our experiences far better than we do. We are exactly the persons God created us to be.

This month we will consider some important questions you may be asking yourself—questions having to do with your relationship with God, your relationships with others, and even your relationship with yourself. It is my hope that these questions will help you to stretch and grow in many ways, especially in your faith.

God, whatever my questions are, I ask you not only to reveal the answers but also to give me the assurance that you hold those answers for me until I am able to understand. Amen.

MAY 2 DO I HAVE A SPECIAL PURPOSE?

Be happy . . . while you are young, and let your heart give you joy in the days of your youth. Follow the ways of your heart and whatever your eyes see, but know that for all these things God will bring you to judgment. —Ecclesiastes 11:9

The book of Ecclesiastes supposedly was written by a teacher to help his students. In the midst of his talk of judgment is a very important message about the way we use time. We can choose to spend our time any way we want, he says, but we must realize that our ability to manage time determines the quality of our lives.

When we are young, it is easy to make having fun and doing the things we enjoy our top priorities. The writer of Ecclesiastes tells us that these desires are what God intends for us, yet they are not all there is to life. In the midst of having fun, we need to learn to be responsible, to love and care for others, and to fulfill our purpose in the universe—because each one of us has been created for a reason. Why not begin today to discover yours?

Lord, let my day be filled with joy and fun, but also help me to discover your special purpose for me. Amen.

MAY 3 WHAT IS GOD CALLING ME TO DO?

The word of the LORD came to Jonah son of Amittai: "Go to the great city of Nineveh and preach against it, because its wickedness has come up before me." But Jonah ran away from the LORD and headed for Tarshish. He went down to Joppa, where he found a ship bound for that port. After paying the fare, he went aboard and sailed for Tarshish to flee from the LORD . . . But the LORD provided a great fish to swallow Jonah, and Jonah was inside the fish three days and three nights. —Jonah 1:1-3, 17

As a young prophet, Jonah knew that God had given him a message the world needed to hear, but he was afraid they would not take him seriously. After all, he was young. Perhaps someone else would say what he needed to say. Besides, if he didn't share the message, what difference would it make anyway?

When God calls us to do something, it is sort of like a homework assignment: If we don't do it, it will still be there, waiting for us. Like any young person, Jonah thought that running would help, but it didn't. God's intentions followed him wherever he went, even into the belly of a whale.

Is there something you know you should be doing, but you keep putting it off? If it is from God, you will not be at peace until it is done. So go on and get started!

God, as I "sit in the belly of a whale," trying to escape my responsibilities, give me the strength to hear your call and reflect it in my actions today. Amen.

WHAT CAN I LEARN FROM OTHERS ABOUT MY PURPOSE OR CALLING?

Simeon took him in his arms and praised God, saying: "Sovereign Lord, as you have promised, you now dismiss your servant in peace. For my eyes have seen your salvation, which you have prepared in the sight of all people, a light for revelation to the Gentiles and for glory to your people Israel." —Luke 2:28-32

After Jesus was born, Joseph and Mary took him to the temple to be blessed. Even before they made it to the priest, there was an old man, Simeon, who also blessed the baby. Simeon knew that Jesus was sent by God to save his people.

People like Simon—those who reminded Jesus that he was special and that God had called him for a great task—helped to prepare Jesus to fulfill his purpose in saving the world. You see, before Jesus could claim to be the Messiah, there had to be people around him who had that expectation of him.

Who are the people in your life who have told you that you are special? What talents have they seen in you, and how have they been willing to help you cultivate these talents? Remember that God has a purpose for your life, and that God uses other people to help you discover, prepare for, and fulfill this purpose.

Lord, help me to recognize my special task or calling by paying attention to the encouragement of others. Amen.

MAY 5

HOW WILL I BE ABLE TO DO WHAT GOD ASKS OF ME?

Before I formed you in the womb I knew you, before you were born I set you apart; I appointed you as a prophet to the nations. —Jeremiah 1:5

Like Jonah, Jeremiah was a young prophet who had been called to speak. Yet Jeremiah refused because he felt that he was not good enough. God reminded him that he had been created for this purpose. Even as a baby in the womb, Jeremiah had been given by God all that he needed to fulfill his task. God was certain that Jeremiah could do it—and do it well.

Do you have a term paper to finish, a conversation that you know God wants you to have, athletic tryouts to endure, or some other worthy "goal" that you need to accomplish, yet you do not feel that you are ready? Go ahead and do it; God has already given you the ability to succeed—not only in this task, but also in a special calling for which you have been created.

Lord, help me begin to recognize the special purpose you created me for, and give me the assurance I need to fulfill all the goals and dreams you have given me. Amen.

MAY 6

HOW DO I LISTEN FOR GOD?

The LORD said, "Go out and stand on the mountain in the presence of the LORD, for the LORD is about to pass by." Then a great and powerful wind tore the mountains apart and shattered the rocks before the LORD, but the LORD was not in the wind. After the wind there was an earthquake, but the LORD was not in the earthquake. After the earthquake came a fire, but the LORD was not in the fire. And after the fire came a gentle whisper. —1 Kings 19:11-12

When the prophet Samuel was looking for a word from God, he expected to find the voice of God in the big, the loud, the obvious. He expected God to speak on Samuel's terms. And when that didn't happen, he thought surely he would encounter God in the midst of a fire. It wasn't until Samuel stopped looking at the phenomena of life that he heard God. And God didn't speak in a grand voice but in a gentle whisper. Samuel had to listen closely in order to hear God speak.

God speaks to us today in many ways. Even though we can see God in the big things and in the crisis events, God also speaks through the small, everyday things, such as a routine prayer time—a time when we are willing to stop and listen.

Dear God, I see you in so many things, big and small. Help me to hear you in my regular prayer time. Amen.

MAY 7 DOES GOD EVER SPEAK TO ME THROUGH MY DREAMS?

So Jacob was left alone, and a man wrestled with him till daybreak. So Jacob called the place Peniel, saying, "It is because I saw God face to face, and yet my life was spared." —Genesis 32:24, 30

Jacob stole the inheritance of the firstborn from his twin brother. And when his brother, Esau, confronted him about it, Jacob ran away. Later he had the dream we read about in today's scripture, and it was through this dream that he received a message from God.

No one really won the battle in Jacob's dream; the angel just got tired of the fight and stopped. When Jacob woke up, his hip was out of socket. Jacob's dream had not been an illusion; it had been a real struggle. In a way, Jacob *was* victorious because God was able to give him an answer to the conflict with his brother, Esau. Upon Jacob's return home, the feud that had lasted for years and had caused such hard feelings was resolved. The families of Jacob and Esau were reconciled and lived as brotherly tribes again.

Is there a conflict so deep in your life that you are dreaming about the answer? The answer to your conflict may not be obvious, but your dreams may be showing you the path.

God, in the midst of my dreams, help me to be willing to walk with you until I am sure of your voice. And if your voice is not to be heard in my dream, give me the wisdom and discernment to know the truth. Amen.

MAY 8

WHY DO I SEEM TO SEE THINGS DIFFERENTLY FROM OTHERS?

He made it known by sending his angel to his servant John, who testifies to everything he saw—that is, the word of God and the testimony of Jesus Christ.
—Revelation 1:1-2

The book of Revelation is a vision revealed to John by God. One characteristic of visions is that they are clear only to the persons who see them. Even today there is debate about what John was talking about. Was this a dream he had? Was he talking figuratively or literally about something that would happen—either in his lifetime or in a future time? The beauty of Revelation is that John cared to share his vision with others. We can look into it and see many of our own situations in John's thoughts.

Have you been thinking about something that no one else sees clearly? Are you reluctant to share your "vision" because you are afraid no one will understand it? Perhaps it was given only to you, so that you will share it with the rest of the world. Remember, all progress in life starts with a vision.

Lord, as I grow up and see things differently, help me to prayerfully follow my vision, for I may be helping the world. Amen.

MAY 9

IS IT OKAY TO STRIVE TO BE THE BEST?

But they kept quiet because on the way they had argued about who was the greatest. Sitting down, Jesus called the Twelve and said, "If anyone wants to be first, he must be the very last, and the servant of all."
—Mark 9:34-35

It seems we are always competing to see who is the best. We compete in school, in extracurricular activities, in sports, in the workplace, and sometimes even in our own homes. There is nothing wrong with striving to be *your best* at whatever you do—a contest with yourself, so to speak. But striving to be *the best*—to be recognized as better than others—can be a dangerous thing.

Jesus' disciples wanted to know who was the greatest among them, and this contest caused much strife in the group. Jesus explained to them that, ultimately, life is not about who is the greatest. In fact, that type of striving will get you nowhere. If you want to be the best in God's eyes, you must be willing to help *all* in the group be the best they can be. It is in their gratitude that you will be rewarded.

Lord, help me strive to do my best—not to be the best. And help me to be more concerned about helping others to win than trying to win myself. Amen.

WHAT IS THE REAL MEASURE OF SUCCESS?

Jesus answered, "If you want to be perfect, go, sell your possessions and give to the poor, and you will have treasure in heaven. Then come, follow me." When the young man heard this, he went away sad, because he had great wealth.
—Matthew 19:21-22

We are constantly getting messages that success means having lots of money, lots of things, and lots of influence over people. Here was a young man who had achieved all of that; yet Jesus told him that if he really wanted to be successful, he needed to get rid of all he had. Jesus was telling him that success in life is not found in what we are able to *get;* it is found in what we are able to *give away*.

We all have those things in life we value—whether they be material possessions or hobbies or goals we want to achieve. But what good are these things if they keep us from committing ourselves completely to Jesus Christ? Can these things ever be the source of real happiness and joy? In a world that values things, how do we learn to value faith?

God, help me to keep my focus on Jesus in the midst of a materialistic world. Amen.

HOW HAS GOD BLESSED ME?

Praise the LORD, O my soul, and forget not all his benefits . . . who satisfies your desires with good things so that your youth is renewed like the eagle's.
—Psalm 103:2, 5

There is a hymn that includes the line "I will lift you up on eagle's wings," which reminds us that God is always our strength and our support. God wants us to go as far as we can in life, and God is willing to carry us all the way. God does this by "feeding" us with blessings in life that make us joyful and healthy. God sends us friends and family, who are our support; teachers, both in school and in life, who give us wisdom; dreams and visions, which drive us into the future.

Make a list of all of the blessings that God has given you—all the good things in your life—and let your gratitude for those things carry you through the day.

Lord, today I am renewed in spirit as I think of all of the good things that you have given me in life. Amen.

HOW CAN I MAKE THE MOST OF THIS DAY?

Be very careful, then, how you live—not as unwise but as wise, making the most of every opportunity. . . . Therefore do not be foolish, but understand what the Lord's will is. —Ephesians 5:15-17

Every day is a gift from God. God has a plan for each of us, and God knows what things are best suited for us; but God has given each of us the ability to co-create our lives. That means that we participate in determining not only *what* we will do but also *how* we will do those things.

Today you will spend time doing some things you must do, but there also is time for doing some things you want to do. Try to find a good balance between the two. Use your "free time" wisely. Plan to make the most of whatever opportunities you may have today. And most important, set aside some time for asking what the Lord's will is for you today.

Lord, help me to become aware of the opportunities that you have given me today, and help me to seek your guidance for how to make the best use of those opportunities. Amen.

HOW CAN I RESIST TEMPTATION?

Jesus, full of the Holy Spirit, returned from the Jordan and was led by the Spirit in the desert, where for forty days he was tempted by the devil. —Luke 4:1-2a

When Jesus went into the desert, the devil tempted him with some self-serving desires. Jesus wanted to tell the world about God's love for us, but he also wanted to become great. Jesus wanted to show the world that we can trust God completely, but he also wanted to test whether or not he had God's special protection. Yet Jesus did not give in to these temptations; he "fought back" with the power of God's Word, and he was victorious.

When we give in to our desires, many times we say that "the devil made me do it," as if we are puppets on a string. The truth is, we *choose* whether or not to give in to temptation. Jesus came into the world to help us understand that no matter how convincing temptation may be, God equips us to see the truth and resist *any* temptation.

If you want to resist temptation, *get into God's Word* and *pray daily*, asking the Holy Spirit to give you wisdom and strength.

Lord, equip me today to resist whatever temptations I may face. Amen.

MAY 14 ARE THERE SOME THINGS THAT CANNOT BE FORGIVEN?

When Jesus saw their faith, he said to the paralytic, "Son, your sins are forgiven."
—Mark 2:5

When Jesus saw this man, he did not address the man's physical condition; he addressed the condition of the man's heart. He told the man that his sins were forgiven. In other words, he was free to let go of whatever was holding him down and preventing him from going forward in life.

Sometimes we allow our sins, mistakes, and negative thoughts to hold us down. Instead of accepting Jesus' forgiveness and moving on, we "beat ourselves up" by replaying the past.

Is there something you are "beating yourself up" over? Whatever it is, Jesus is telling you that it is okay to let go of it. Jesus loves you so much that he is willing to forgive *all* your sins. Nothing can "disqualify" you from receiving his incredible love and grace. Once you've admitted a sin and decided to turn away from it, then *let it go*. Accept Jesus' forgiveness and never look back.

Jesus, on this day, help me come to understand, like the paralytic, that my sins are forgiven and I can move on. Amen.

CAN JESUS REALLY BE MY FRIEND?

After six days Jesus took Peter, James and John with him and led them up a high mountain, where they were all alone. There he was transfigured before them. . . . Then a cloud appeared and enveloped them, and a voice came from the cloud: "This is my Son, whom I love. Listen to him!" —Mark 9:2, 7

This was one of the most intimate times of Jesus' life. It was a time when Jesus went on the mountain to pray, to speak with God. Yet he took his closest friends with him. Usually we think of prayer as a time when we are alone with God and God responds directly to us. In this instance, however, God did not direct his words to Jesus; he spoke to the friends Jesus had brought with him. By bringing along his friends for this intimate moment, Jesus also brought along all of us who understand him to be our Lord and Savior. The words God shared with Peter, James, and John are shared with all of us: "This is my beloved Son. . . . Listen to him!"

Jesus wants to be your closest, most trusted friend. He has so much to give you, so much to teach you. *Listen* to him.

Thank you, Christ, for loving me enough to bring me into the intimate relationship between you and God. Help me to listen to all you have to teach me. Amen.

WHO CAN HELP ME GROW IN MY FAITH?

When they had crossed, Elijah said to Elisha, "Tell me, what can I do for you before I am taken from you?" "Let me inherit a double portion of your spirit," Elisha replied. —2 Kings 2:9

Elijah was taken up to heaven in a whirlwind (2 Kings 2:11), yet Elijah knew that he was human and that humans do not live on this Earth forever. He knew he needed a student to whom he could teach everything he knew, so that his good would live on past the years of his humanity. He chose Elisha. When it was time for Elijah to leave this world, he wanted to give Elisha something to remember him by. Elisha asked for a double portion of Elijah's spirit. His dream was to be capable of everything that his teacher was capable of, and then some.

Do you have someone in your life you consider to be a spiritual mentor— someone who encourages and helps you to grow in faith? If not, ask God to provide one for you. And when this person becomes apparent, do all that you can to learn from his or her example. If you earnestly desire and seek to grow in faith, God *will* give you a double portion!

Dear God, help me to learn all I can from the spiritual mentors you provide, so that I may grow in faith and wisdom. Amen.

WHAT IS MY HERITAGE?

And Joseph made the sons of Israel swear an oath and said, "God will surely come to your aid, and then you must carry my bones up from this place." —Genesis 50:25

Joseph's last words to his sons instructed them to take his bones with them when they left Egypt and returned home to the land of his birth. When I hear this story, I think of my grandmother, who passed on some of her special belongings to me when she died. Though she is gone, I know that she still lives through me. I carry my memory of her with me each day, and it reminds me that I have a heritage—I have a sense of belonging. But even more important, it reminds me that the past has a place in the future—*in me*. You see, I have the opportunity to achieve everything she would have wanted for me. I also have the opportunity to pass on my heritage. And I will pass it on to my children, so that they, too, can carry the "bones" of our ancestors into our inherited promised land.

Lord, I have a heritage, a heritage that has been continued for generations. Help me to create a future worthy of continuing this heritage. Amen.

WHY DO CERTAIN FAMILY MEMBERS IRRITATE ME SO MUCH?

As Jesus and his disciples were on their way, he came to a village where a woman named Martha opened her home to him. She had a sister called Mary, who sat at the Lord's feet listening to what he said. But Martha was distracted by all the preparations that had to be made. She came to him and asked, "Lord, don't you care that my sister has left me to do the work by myself? Tell her to help me!"
—Luke 10:38-40

Have you ever considered what kind of relationship these two sisters may have had? Here's my take on it.

Martha was the quiet one, always doing what she was supposed to do. Mary was the bubbly one, always getting in trouble because she was "goofing off." Martha secretly admired her sister's outgoing nature, yet she was jealous of it too. Likewise, Mary respected her sister for always trying to do the right thing, yet she couldn't help resenting her for it; she wanted to learn what was right too.

On this day, they had the chance to let their personalities work together. While one prepared food for their guest, Jesus, the other could use her people skills to entertain him. The things they resented most about each other could be complementary, making them the perfect team—*if only they were willing to work together.*

What do you resent most about each person in your family? As you notice these things, observe how your personalities actually fit together like pieces of a puzzle. Think about the ways you complement one another and work for a common cause.

Dear Lord, thank you for the team you have given me called family. In the midst of our struggles, help us to see how we can work together and make the most of our differences. Amen.

MAY 19 — WHAT KIND OF RELATIONSHIP SHOULD I HAVE WITH MY SIBLINGS?

Then the LORD said to Cain, "Where is your brother Abel?" "I don't know," he replied. "Am I my brother's keeper?" —Genesis 4:9

Two sisters go to the same high school. Cindy is a freshman; Lindsey is a senior. Lindsey thinks Cindy embarrasses her in front of all her friends. One day Lindsey sees Cindy being teased in the lunch room, but she doesn't do anything about it. Later when someone asks why Lindsey didn't defend her sister, Lindsey just shrugs it off and says, "I'm not my sister's keeper."

That's what Cain said about his brother, Abel. Cain felt he was not responsible for his brother, yet he was responsible for killing him! Most relationships between siblings do not lead to such violent ends—and thankfully so! But consider this: How do the things that happen in our homes affect the way we treat our siblings in school, at church, and in other public places?

The truth is, we *are* our brothers' and sisters' keepers. God has given us the responsibility and *privilege* of helping them, encouraging them, and seeing them through the ups and downs of life.

Lord, please help me to be the kind of brother or sister I need to be—today and always. Amen.

AS I GROW IN FAITH, DO I RISK LOSING SOME OF THE RELATIONSHIPS IN MY LIFE?

Afterward Moses and Aaron went to Pharaoh and said, "This is what the LORD, the God of Israel, says: 'Let my people go, so that they may hold a festival to me in the desert.'" Pharaoh said, "Who is the LORD, that I should obey him and let Israel go? I do not know the LORD and I will not let Israel go." —Exodus 5:1-2

Moses and Pharaoh were raised in the same household. They shared the same family and the same beliefs from childhood. But one day, after they had grown up, they stood in opposition to each other. No matter how much they talked, they could not find common ground. And as they looked at the same "picture," they saw different things. One saw the children of Israel as a means to help him show the world that he was a great person; the other came to realize that these slaves were indeed his brothers and sisters.

As Moses' faith grew, he lost his relationship with the one he had known as his brother, but he gained a whole new family—a family of faith. Likewise, as our faith matures, we sometimes lose relationships with those who see things differently than we do. But we can trust God to heal our hearts and give us new relationships to "fill the gaps" in our lives.

God, help me to know that as I grow up and mature in my faith, some things will change—but only because you are preparing me to take a long exodus out of childhood into adulthood. Amen.

WILL MY FRIEND EVER BE ABLE TO FORGIVE ME?

Peter declared, "Even if all fall away, I will not." "I tell you the truth," Jesus answered, "today—yes, tonight—before the rooster crows twice you yourself will disown me three times." —Mark 14:29-30

Our friends can always depend on us in their time of need, right? Peter thought the same thing—until he heard the rooster crow.

There is a point in all of us when our fears can cause us to desert the people we love. Something may happen to a friend, and we may be afraid to get involved. Like Peter, we may even publicly deny, belittle, or condemn our friend. But because of Jesus Christ, we have the hope of reconciliation and restoration. Even though Peter abandoned Jesus, Jesus forgave him and gave him the opportunity to affirm his love for Jesus (see John 21:15-17). Peter and Jesus remained friends. And Peter treasured all of the things he had experienced with Jesus enough to share them with all the world.

Do you need to seek the forgiveness of a friend you have "betrayed" in some way? Don't put it off. Don't let fear cause you to make yet another mistake.

Lord, please forgive me for failing my friend, and help my friend to forgive me as well. I know that I will always have limitations and fears, but I ask you to help me overcome them so that I may become a true friend. Amen.

MAY 22 — WHAT DOES IT MEAN TO BE LOYAL?

But Ruth replied, "Don't urge me to leave you or to turn back from you. Where you go I will go, and where you stay I will stay. Your people will be my people and your God my God. Where you die I will die, and there I will be buried. May the LORD deal with me, be it ever so severely, if anything but death separates you and me." —Ruth 1:16, 17

Ruth's relationship with her mother-in-law, Naomi, was special. Even when Ruth's husband died and Naomi encouraged her to go on with her life, Ruth pledged to stay with Naomi no matter what. Although their relationship was not established through birth, they loved each other dearly. Theirs was a love that demonstrated the true meaning of commitment and loyalty. And it was this love that started a nation.

You see, eventually Naomi returned to her homeland with Ruth, and Ruth married and had a son—a son whose name would head the list of a very important family tree. Because Ruth was not willing to abandon Naomi, the lineage of both King David and Jesus Christ was established.

Think of the important relationships in your life—relationships with your family as well as your friends. How can you demonstrate loyalty in each of these relationships?

Dear Lord, help me to be loyal to those I love—to put their best interests above my own—both now as well as in the future. Amen.

WHAT IS A TRUE FRIENDSHIP?

Then Herod and his soldiers ridiculed and mocked him. Dressing him in an elegant robe, they sent him back to Pilate. That day Herod and Pilate became friends—before this they had been enemies.

—Luke 23:11-12

We usually think of friends as people with whom we have something in common, yet *true friends help us grow in a positive way.* Friendships can be a wonderful part of life, but they also can be dangerous if they are based on the wrong things. When a relationship is based on violence, drugs, illegal activities, gossip, cruel behavior, or other harmful things, is that really a friendship—or is it just a mutually beneficial arrangement?

Herod and Pilate did not become "friends" until after Jesus' death. They actually hated each other before they discovered a common bond—a bond that stemmed from their participation in the crucifixion of Jesus. Was theirs a true friendship?

It is very easy to have a destructive relationship, especially if you see some benefit in it. But ask yourself this question: In the long run, where will it lead me?

Are all the people I call friends really good for me? Are they helping me grow in a positive way? If not, Lord, help me to rethink my friendships. Amen.

WHAT IS A "BEST FRIEND"?

And Jonathan had David reaffirm his oath out of love for him, because he loved him as he loved himself.   *—1 Samuel 20:17*

Jonathan was the son of the King. David was a young soldier who would become one of the King's worst enemies. Yet these two became the best of friends. Through the years, their friendship went through many trials. Yet through it all, David never forgot his oath of love to his friend.

Before Jonathan died, he had the opportunity to protect David with his life. In return, when Jonathan's whole family was executed, David took in Jonathan's young son and raised him as his own. Friendships this deep are few and far between.

Do you have a friend who has stuck with you "forever"? What friend would stand by you with his or her very life? Have you taken the time to acknowledge this person's love for you? If something threatened to come between you, what would you do to save your friendship?

Dear Lord, today I lift my best friend to you in prayer and ask for his/her continued protection and well-being. Amen.

CAN I SEE GOD IN MY DATING RELATIONSHIPS?

Love is patient, love is kind. It does not envy, it does not boast, it is not proud. It is not rude, it is not self-seeking, it is not easily angered, it keeps no record of wrongs. Love does not delight in evil but rejoices with the truth. It always trusts, always hopes, always perseveres. —1 Corinthians 13:4-7

Dating can be a fun way to get to know other people and to learn about life—even about yourself. As a relationship grows, the other person becomes a special part of your life. You may even wonder what kind of future you may have with this person. Will you be friends, or maybe more?

A relationship that helps us see the love of God is a relationship with a future, no matter what that future may be. This passage from 1 Corinthians describes the love that God has for us—and that we are to have for others. The relationships in our lives should be reflections of God's love. Though none of us is perfect or capable of God's perfect love, we can strive to be imitators of God's love.

There is much more to a relationship than physical attraction, status, and other shallow concerns. As you date, pay attention to see if your feelings and actions are a reflection of the love of God.

Lord, as I begin dating, let my relationships be a reflection of you. Help me and the persons I date to seek the reflection of your love in all that we do together. Amen.

AM I "RUSHING THINGS" IN RELATIONSHIPS WITH THE OPPOSITE SEX?

Scarcely had I passed them when I found the one my heart loves. I held him and would not let him go till I had brought him to my mother's house, to the room of the one who conceived me. Daughters of Jerusalem, I charge you by the gazelles and by the does of the field: Do not arouse or awaken love until it so desires. —Song of Songs 3:4-5

The Song of Songs is a beautiful love poem. In these verses, the woman talks of bringing her future husband to her mother's home—an act that would have demonstrated the purity of their love. Then she talks about the nature of true love, telling the daughters of Jerusalem that sexual intimacy should not be rushed. In so many words, she is explaining that love and lust are not the same. Or, as the familiar saying goes, "True love waits."

There's no doubt that God created us to experience physical intimacy, which is why we have such an intense desire for it. Yet God also ordained a beautiful way for us to fulfill that desire: marriage. In Genesis 2:24 we read, "For this reason a man will leave his father and mother and be united to his wife, and they will become one flesh."

Like anything of great value, sexual intimacy is worth waiting for.

Dear Lord, as I learn more about what to look for in a relationship with the opposite sex, give me the patience not to rush things before their time. Help me to remember that saving physical intimacy for marriage is okay—after all, it's what you intended from the very start. Amen.

MAY 27 CAN PEER PRESSURE EVER BE A GOOD THING?

He said, "Look! I see four men walking around in the fire, unbound and unharmed, and the fourth looks like a son of the gods."
—Daniel 3:25

When we think of peer pressure, we usually think of friends persuading us to do things we shouldn't do. But peer pressure also can be a positive thing. The story of Shadrach, Meshach, and Abednego is the ultimate story of peer pressure because it shows us both kinds.

These three young men had been taken into captivity and were expected to give up all they had been raised to believe was right. They were locked in a furnace, waiting to be burned, because they refused to give up their heritage and religious beliefs. Yet as they stuck together, God gave them the strength to withstand the pressure to change. Not only did they have one another; Christ was present in the midst of their relationships, helping them keep their faith in God.

When was the last time you depended on your friends to keep you strong so that you could do the right thing?

Today I lift up my friends who have been in the "pressure cooker" with me and have helped me keep my faith in the midst of the heat. Amen.

MAY 28
WHEN I'M MAD AT SOMEONE, WHAT DOES GOD WANT ME TO DO?

If your brother sins against you, go and show him his fault, just between the two of you. If he listens to you, you have won your brother over.
—Matthew 18:15

How many times this week has someone gotten on your nerves? How many times has someone *purposely* done something to get on your nerves? Have you ever noticed that when you are mad at someone, it is hard to function at school or work or wherever you may find yourself? When you let it slide, things just seem to get worse. The person usually does something else to irritate you, and you just get madder and madder. One way or another, you always seem to be pulled back into the pit of anger.

It's so true: When we're mad at someone, we're mad at the world. Have you ever thought about telling that someone why you are mad? Have you ever thought about trying to make peace with him or her? Try it today, and see if it changes your outlook on life.

Lord, help me to share my feelings with those I am angry or upset with today, and help them to listen to what I have to say. Amen.

MAY 29
WHAT SHOULD I DO WHEN I'M AFRAID?

But when they saw him walking on the lake, they thought he was a ghost. They cried out, because they all saw him and were terrified. Immediately he spoke to them and said, "Take courage! It is I. Don't be afraid."
—Mark 6:49-50

"Don't be afraid" has been the greeting of many angels as they have come into the lives of humans. Christ also came into our lives to share this message. The disciples saw firsthand that Jesus was in control of all the world—even the wind and the sea. They were afraid because what they saw was out of the ordinary. But Jesus told them there was no need to fear; he was in control, and he was right there with them.

Going through a scary or difficult time and being afraid go hand in hand. But, like the disciples, we don't have to be afraid. We can remember that Jesus is still in control, and he's right here with us, working in our lives—sometimes in ways that are way "out of the ordinary." Best of all, the Bible assures us that after the fear, there will be joy.

Look around. God is at work in your life. Take courage, and don't be afraid!

Lord, as I go through my day, help me to understand your greeting to me in life: "Don't be afraid." Amen.

WHAT DO I DO WHEN I'VE LOST HOPE?

Early the next morning Abraham took some food and a skin of water and gave them to Hagar. He set them on her shoulders and then sent her off with the boy. She went on her way and wandered in the desert of Beersheba. When the water in the skin was gone, she put the boy under one of the bushes. Then she went off and sat down nearby, about a bowshot away, for she thought, "I cannot watch the boy die." And as she sat there nearby, she began to sob. —Genesis 21:14-16

Hagar's mistress, Sarah, had always been willing to support her. But the baby, Ishmael, was a threat to Sarah's son, Isaac. So Sarah, Abraham's wife, kicked both mother and son out of the house.

Now Hagar sat alone in the desert. Her first thought was to abandon the baby. In the midst of her despair, God spoke to her and told her not to worry. Even though she was young and inexperienced, she was a mother now, and Ishmael depended on her. If it wasn't for God's assurance of support in the midst of the wilderness, Ishmael would not have been raised to become the father of a mighty nation.

God also speaks to us in the midst of our "wilderness experiences." Next time you've lost all hope, don't act impulsively. Stop and listen for God's guidance. Though you may not *hear* an answer, you can be sure that God will respond in just the way you need.

Lord, in the midst of my "wilderness experience," let your voice be my guidepost. Amen.

MAY 31

CAN I REALLY MAKE A DIFFERENCE?

And afterward, I will pour out my Spirit on all people. Your sons and daughters will prophesy, your old men will dream dreams, your young men will see visions. —Joel 2:28

Joel wrote these words to encourage the people of Israel. In the midst of war, it seemed that nothing had been accomplished because everyone had been too preoccupied with the crisis. Everyone had been so caught up in the *now* that they had given no thought to the future.

Joel's message for us today is to always keep our eyes on the future. Your parents, teachers, and other adults have dreams of what needs to be done in the world. As you become more aware of these dreams and aspirations, you are contributing your own ideas and shaping your own dreams about a better world. It is up to you to begin making these dreams become the reality of the future. All people of all ages help to create the future, but your generation will take over where others have left off. You *can* make a difference. Dream on!

Lord, help me to continue dreaming of a better world, and show me the steps I can take to make those dreams realities. Amen.

JUNE

MAKING
WISE
CHOICES

Kwasi Kena

JUNE

MAKING WISE CHOICES

Kwasi Kena

JUNE 1

LEARN GODLY WISDOM

The proverbs of Solomon son of David, king of Israel: for attaining wisdom and discipline; for understanding words of insight; for acquiring a disciplined and prudent life, doing what is right and just and fair; for giving prudence to the simple, knowledge and discretion to the young.
—Proverbs 1:1-4

Families often use proverbs to teach important lessons. My grandmother used to say, "Hard times will make a monkey eat red pepper." Those few words reminded me to make adjustments in difficult times. People with godly wisdom have much to teach us. Solomon was such a man.

Scripture describes Solomon as the wisest man who ever lived (see 1 Kings 4:29-34). God blessed him with tremendous insights about life. He wrote much of this wisdom down in the form of proverbs. Proverbs teach us better ways of dealing with everyday situations. They teach us discipline, morality, and plain old good sense. This month, we'll explore the theme "making wise choices" by examining some important biblical proverbs. Take time to think and meditate on them. You'll be surprised at how useful they can be in your life.

Dear Lord, direct me to godly people full of wisdom who will teach me how to be wise and just and fair. Amen.

JUNE 2

HAVE ZERO TOLERANCE

Wine is a mocker and beer a brawler; whoever is led astray by them is not wise.
—Proverbs 20:1

Gary and his friends were a few days away from their high school graduation. They often spent their lunch hour sitting in Teddy's car in the school parking lot dreaming about college, summer jobs, or new cars. One day as lunch hour was almost over, Teddy pulled out a six pack. "Let's get a quick buzz before we go back," he said with a grin.

Gary had never had beer before, and soon his friends "made" him guzzle down three in a row. The last beer went down too fast, and Gary choked a little. While he was coughing, he accidentally spilled beer on Teddy's favorite shirt. "You're gonna pay for this!" yelled Teddy. One thing led to another, and the little beer party turned into a brawl just as the principal was driving up. Everyone froze; they knew they attended a "zero tolerance" school. Drinking on school property meant expulsion.

Dear Lord, give me the will and good sense to avoid taking any substance that alters my good judgment. Amen.

JUNE 3 STAY SHARP! CHOOSE GOOD FRIENDS!

Iron sharpens iron, and one person sharpens the wits of another.
—Proverbs 27:17 (NRSV)

Marvin and Mel went everywhere together. Years ago, when they played on the same soccer team, people started calling them M & M. Marvin came from a large family. All of his brothers and sisters helped around the house. Marvin knew how to cook dinner, wash clothes, and repair small electrical appliances. Each time Mel visited Marvin, he learned something new. That was good, because Mel, who was a little spoiled, learned how to cook a few meals and clean up behind himself.

Mel's family was small, and his dad was a computer whiz. When Marvin visited their house, Mel and his dad showed Marvin how to maneuver around the computer. Before he knew it, Marvin was surfing the Internet for information about his favorite baseball team.

Mel and Marvin were good influences on each other. Like iron sharpens iron, good friendships keep us from being dull.

Dear Lord, lead me to people who are good influences on my life. May our friendships keep us sharp. Amen.

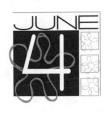

STAND UP FOR WHAT IS RIGHT

Speak up for those who cannot speak for themselves, for the rights of all who are destitute. Speak up and judge fairly; defend the rights of the poor and needy. —Proverbs 31:8-9

Jimmy was never very athletic. He and his thick "coke bottle" glasses were always poking around seldom-used books and journals in the library. He was the type of guy who wondered about things like the chemical make-up of maple syrup or single-celled organisms on Mars. Jimmy's classmates never tired of playing practical jokes on him.

One day Marty, the wrestling team captain, witnessed a terrible thing happening in the cafeteria. As Jimmy was walking past the tables where all of the "popular" students ate, someone intentionally tripped him. Marty cringed as Jimmy's expensive glasses shattered on the floor. Meanwhile, Jimmy's tray of food flew into the air and came down on Melissa's new outfit. Her boyfriend, Jerry, started yelling and pushing Jimmy. If someone didn't do something, Jimmy was going to get hurt.

Scripture invites us to defend people in need. What can you do for someone today?

Dear Lord, give me the courage to stand up for what is right— even when it's unpopular. Amen.

SPEAK PLEASANT WORDS

Pleasant words are a honeycomb, sweet to the soul and healing to the bones. —Proverbs 16:24

Whenever Betty's grandmother called, she'd say, "How's Grandma's girl?" and Betty knew everything was all right. Her Gram was also a great cook. She and Betty spent many hours making cookies and muffins together. That's why it was so devastating when her Gram had a stroke and had to go to a nursing home.

For a long time, Betty refused to go and visit. "I just can't stand to see Gram in a nursing home," she moaned. Deep inside, Betty feared that Gram wouldn't recognize her anymore. Betty's mother interrupted her thoughts, saying, "But if you were sick, don't you think Gram would see about you?" Finally, Betty decided to visit Gram. As soon as she walked into her grandmother's room, Gram formed a weak smile and said, "How's Grandma's girl?"

Soon Betty began to share what had happened to her that day. They spent hours enjoying each other's company.

Dear Lord, encourage me to speak pleasant, healing words to someone today. Amen.

JUNE 6 ASK YOURSELF, "WHAT WOULD JESUS DO?"

The name of the LORD is a strong tower; the righteous run to it and are safe.
—*Proverbs 18:10*

Billy and his friends loved to joke and pull pranks on people. Most of the time their jokes were harmless, and everyone got a big laugh. At other times, their jokes crossed the line, and people got hurt. They especially liked to pick on people who were "different" in some way.

They teased Frank because he took dance lessons. They harassed Tracy because she dressed in second-hand clothing. Billy never thought twice about giving people a hard time until he saw Sidney wearing a bracelet with the letters WWJD on it.

"What's that, Sid?" Billy asked.

"Oh, this is something I wear to remind me to ask the question *What would Jesus do?* before I say or do anything. I kinda' like it, cuz it helps me think about doing something positive for people."

Sid's comment challenged Billy to think about how he should be treating people.

Jesus, may the mention of your name remind me to fill my thoughts with your love and concern for others. Amen.

JUNE 7 CONSIDER YOUR MOTIVES

All one's ways may be pure in one's own eyes, but the LORD weighs the spirit.
—*Proverbs 16:2 (NRSV)*

"What's the big deal?" Chrissy whined. "Nobody got hurt."

Chrissy was trying to explain to her parents why the department store manager called them to the security office. It seemed that Chrissy had bought a dress, wore it for graduation, and then tried to return it for a refund. The only problem in her plan was that the store clerk happened to see Chrissy wearing the dress on graduation night. To make matters worse, Chrissy had spilled some cola on the dress and had to get it dry-cleaned. The dry cleaning receipt was in the bag with the dress when she tried to return it.

When Chrissy threatened to sue the store or somehow publicly embarrass them, the clerk called security. Now, Chrissy sat in front of her parents, humiliated.

Our actions may seem innocent, but God looks at our motives.

Dear Lord, your ways are greater than my ways; help me to act on pure and godly motives. Amen.

 # JUNE 8 DON'T GET LEFT BEHIND— WORK HARD!

A little sleep, a little slumber, a little folding of the hands to rest, and poverty will come upon you like a robber, and want, like an armed warrior.
— *Proverbs 6:10-11 (NRSV)*

"Get up, Pete! You're gonna be late!" Every school day, Pete's mom begged him to get up. When he finally trudged to school, he did just enough to get by. There was one thing about school Pete enjoyed, though— being the class clown. It was intoxicating. When everyone laughed at his pranks, Pete felt like he was on a natural high. When the school year ended, no one was surprised when Pete graduated near the bottom of his class.

Now, in the middle of June, Pete sits at home remembering graduation day. Pete's school is one of the best in the state, and many of his friends have earned full scholarships to big schools. Pete still remembers feeling jealous when the crowd applauded after the principal announced each scholarship. "What are you going to do, Pete?" his friends kept asking him. This summer Pete is still trying to answer that question.

Dear Lord, teach me the benefit of hard work—even when I don't feel like doing it. Amen.

JUNE 9 YOUR BODY, GOD'S BODY: TREAT IT WITH RESPECT

Wisdom calls aloud in the street, she raises her voice in the public squares; at the head of the noisy streets she cries out, in the gateways of the city she makes her speech.
—*Proverbs 1:20-21*

"Oh, so it's like that, huh? C'mon! Everybody's doin' it. You know you want to. . . ."

Terry tried every line in the book on his girlfriend, Sherrie, but she wouldn't budge.

"Look," Terry pleaded, "nobody will ever know. I'm not like that. I keep my business to myself."

"I don't care," said Sherrie. "Even if nobody else ever found out, I would know that I'd had sex with you. What good does it do if people think you're one kind of person but you know that it's a lie?"

"Why are you scared?" Terry begged. "I don't have AIDS."

"Look," Sherrie replied, "my sister is a nurse, and she showed me a pamphlet full of *incurable sexual diseases* that some people don't even realize they have for years. AIDS isn't the only incurable sexual disease you can get. I'm just not ready for this, Terry!"

Dear Lord, my body is your body too. Remind me that treating my body with respect honors you. Amen.

JUNE 10 VOLUNTEERING PAYS—TRY IT!

Some give freely, yet grow all the richer; others withhold what is due, and only suffer want. A generous person will be enriched, and one who gives water will get water.
—*Proverbs 11:24-25 (NRSV)*

Have you ever considered volunteer work? Freely giving your time to others yields great rewards. David found that out in an unlikely place—the nursing home.

During the school year, the principal asked David and a few classmates to take some residents of a nearby nursing home to a shopping mall. David met Ross, a sixty-year-old former contractor, confined to a wheelchair.

"I get so lonely," Ross complained. "My family hardly visits."

David shared with Ross that he played guitar. Ross said, "Why don't you come by and play sometime?"

David was very shy, but he decided to give it a try. That Saturday he played for fifteen minutes at the nursing home. David discovered that the more he played, the more he received. The people's eyes expressed their appreciation.

David has no shortage of friends these days; everyone at the nursing home thinks he's the greatest.

Dear Lord, help me to realize the joy that comes from giving in volunteer service to others. Show me where I can freely give some of my time in my community or church. Amen.

STOP ARGUMENTS EARLY

Starting a quarrel is like breaching a dam; so drop the matter before a dispute breaks out. —*Proverbs 17:14*

"Get out of my face, Marty! I didn't take your money!"

Jerry is tired of being accused by his sixteen-year-old younger brother. Marty won't listen to reason because the money he's been saving for a new CD is gone. Without any proof, Marty just started blaming Jerry for his problems. Jerry denies taking the money, but Marty won't let it go.

Still convinced that Jerry is lying, Marty follows him to his part-time job, shouting, "Where's my money, Jerry?" Marty's voice gets louder and louder until the customers start leaving. By then, Jerry has had enough, and he pushes Marty. Marty pushes back, sending Jerry reeling into a glassware display. Infuriated, the store manager kicks Marty out of the store and fires Jerry on the spot.

Back at home, Marty is feeling terrible for what happened. He knows he went too far, but he's not sure how he should have handled the situation. Jerry just sits alone in his room, wondering what he could have done differently to prevent the quarrel from becoming such a major problem.

Dear God, teach me to drop matters before major disputes break out. Amen.

USE YOUR GIFTS FOR GOD

Wisdom is supreme; therefore get wisdom. Though it cost all you have, get understanding. —*Proverbs 4:7*

"How did you get to be so good on the piano?" asked Marsha.

"Well," began her teacher, "you've got to practice until your hands are like steel traps. You need to know how to play a hundred tunes in twelve keys. Listen to everyone you can; play with everyone you can. . . ."

At home, Marsha sat in awe as she listened to her mother describe her preparation for college: "Well, sweetheart, they gave us a suggested reading list of the classics, and I read all of them. I used to work math problems at night for something to do. I realized something, though. God gives all of us talents in different areas. It's up to us to discover and develop those gifts. Then, once you strive for excellence, pray for the wisdom to know how to best use your abilities for God."

"Though it cost all you have, get understanding."

Dear Lord, give me the desire to strive for excellence and the patience to make wise use of my abilities. Amen.

JUNE 13 REMEMBER THAT LOVE DISCIPLINES

My [child], do not despise the LORD's discipline and do not resent his rebuke, because the LORD disciplines those he loves, as a father the son he delights in. —Proverbs 3:11-12

Carey felt terrible. She was grounded from driving for two weeks! Her parents had restricted her after she came home an hour after her curfew—again. "This is just not fair!" she groaned.

Later that night, her favorite aunt, Sharon, came by.

"I think I know how you feel," said Aunt Sharon. "Once, I got into my father's car without his permission. Before I knew it, I had accidentally put the car in reverse and barreled through the neighbor's new fence. My father loved me, but he was very disappointed. He just came out, took the keys, and didn't say anything. He knew that that would make me think about what I did. I realize now that my father loved me enough to try to correct my thoughtless behavior."

God is no different; he disciplines us because he loves us.

Dear God, help me to accept discipline and realize that only a loving person would even bother to correct me. Amen.

AVOID
BAD COMPANY

Make no friends with those given to anger, and do not associate with hotheads, or you may learn their ways and entangle yourself in a snare. —Proverbs 22:24-25 (NRSV)

Though Eric was new in town, he sure got a lot of attention. Both his voice and physique were powerful and intimidating; but it was his temper that people remembered most. He got angry at the smallest things. People just let him bully them because they were afraid of his never-ending need for revenge.

John, who lived next door to Eric, wished he could be popular. Amazingly, he and Eric became friends, and John started imitating Eric's ways. With Eric at his side, John found it easy to manipulate people. Over time, John's reputation was as bad as Eric's was.

John enjoyed his new reputation until he noticed that the few friends he once had now avoided him. One day, he wished out loud that he had his friends back. Eric overheard it and called him a mama's boy. John felt devastated; his new reputation had brought him nothing but trouble.

Dear Lord, give me the wisdom to avoid bad company and the courage to break harmful relationships. Amen.

DEVELOP DISCIPLINE

The fear of the LORD is the beginning of knowledge, but fools despise wisdom and discipline. —Proverbs 1:7

One night at youth fellowship, Larry's youth pastor said that Christians need to develop discipline because discipline is a mark of discipleship. "Name any great person," he said, "and you'll discover discipline in his or her life."

Two days later, Larry and his friend Phil were at a gym. They stared in amazement at a local body builder.

"I'd give anything to look like that," Larry said.

"No, you wouldn't!" interrupted the voice of a stranger.

"What do you mean?" asked Larry. "That guy is built and probably gets all the ladies."

The stranger came over and sat down beside Larry and Phil to explain.

"I'm his weight training coach," the stranger said. "I see you young guys come in here all the time. You want his body, but you don't want his discipline. He lifts five days a week, eats a special diet, and listens to correction. Are you ready for that?"

What about you? God needs disciples who aren't afraid of discipline.

Dear Lord, my life needs discipline and direction. Show me what it means to be your disciple. Amen.

JUNE 16 CHOOSE YOUR FRIENDS CAREFULLY

The righteous gives good advice to friends, but the way of the wicked leads astray.
—Proverbs 12:26 (NRSV)

Myra couldn't understand why her parents were so nosey. They always wanted to know everything about her friends. While she was in the middle of a major pouting episode, her sister Rita came home from her first semester of college. Boy, did she have some stories to tell!

It seems that some of Rita's girlfriends discovered a way to tap into the school's long distance service. That semester, students illegally charged to the college over $50,000 worth of calls. Everyone involved was put on probation and ordered to pay a percentage of the outstanding bill. Rita also told Myra about several girls who had listened to some smooth-talking guys who deserted them after infecting them with AIDS.

"I don't want to sound like Mom and Dad, Myra, but you really have to be careful about who you hang out with," explained Rita.

Proverbs 12:26 encourages us to be cautious in friendship.

Dear Lord, help me to take my time in choosing good friends. Lead me to people who are pleasing in your sight. Amen.

JUNE 17 PRACTICE SELF-CONTROL

Fools show their anger at once, but the prudent ignore an insult.
—Proverbs 12:16 (NRSV)

"You just *performed* today, didn't you!"

Larry's mom was hot. Larry had gotten into the worst fight of his life. He and a couple of friends were sitting around in a fast food restaurant when it started. Larry overheard part of a conversation that his friend Nicky was having at another table. Larry somehow thought Nicky had said something about Larry's girlfriend. That made Larry go berserk. He started calling Nicky names until they finally wound up outside, rolling in the street.

They just went on and on until the police drove up and arrested Larry.

He was eighteen. If the court found him guilty of assault, it would stay on his record—for life. The sad thing is, it turned out that Nicky was talking about somebody else.

A few moments of patience can save you a lifetime of trouble. Be strong! Practice self-control.

Dear Lord, teach me how to overlook insults and show Christian maturity through self-control. Amen.

HONOR JESUS IN ALL YOU DO

A good name is more desirable than great riches; to be esteemed is better than silver or gold. —Proverbs 22:1

I live in Ghana, West Africa, where my wife and I serve as teaching missionaries. One thing that fascinates us in Ghana is the tremendous emphasis that their culture places on respect for others. If a person is even one day older than you are, you must respect that person as your elder. People treat the elderly very kindly because gray hair is a sign of wisdom If you are named after a grandparent, uncle, aunt, or other relative, people put the title *nana* in front of your name. Nana is a term of respect. It also reminds the person to live honorably out of respect for his or her relative. As followers of Christ, we can learn something from this practice.

We should think of the term *Christian* as a title of respect. Each time you say, "I am a Christian," it should remind you to honor Jesus through godly living.

Dear Lord, as I proclaim to be a Christian, help me to carry that title as a reminder of your love and sacrifice for me. Help me to honor you with my life today. Amen.

LEARN TO HOLD YOUR TONGUE

When words are many, sin is not absent, but [one] who holds [the] tongue is wise. —Proverbs 10:19

Vickie sat munching popcorn with her friends until the lights dimmed in the movie theater. Then Vickie started sharing with them every bit of juicy gossip she'd heard.

"Ben broke up with Louise," she said confidently. "It's true; I saw him hugging some 'strange girl' in his car yesterday. I saw them all over town today. I knew he was like that."

Vickie talked during the entire movie. When the movie ended and the lights came back on, Vickie stood to leave. Suddenly, she turned green. Ben and the "strange girl" had been sitting just behind them.

"Hi, Vickie," said Ben sternly. "This is my cousin visiting from California. I haven't seen her in years."

Since Vickie was a child, her mother had said, "If you're always talking, sooner or later a lie will jump out before you can catch it." How Vickie wished now she'd learned to hold her tongue.

Dear Lord, my tongue has the power to hurt or heal. Give me the wisdom to know when to speak and when to be silent. Amen.

JUNE 20 TRUST GOD COMPLETELY

Trust in the LORD with all your heart and lean not on your own understanding; in all your ways acknowledge him, and he will make your paths straight. —Proverbs 3:5-6

Eddie thought all that "Christian stuff" was for sissies until he met Cliff at a Christian Athletes meeting. Cliff had played pro baseball until sustaining a career-ending injury.

"That injury nearly devastated me," Cliff told the crowd. "One day you're a star; the next day you're packing your bags. I sulked for months until our team chaplain encouraged me to start reading the Bible for transformation. 'Cliff,' he said, 'when you read the Bible, let God into your imagination. Become a participant in the Bible story. Imagine the sights, the sounds, the smells, everything. Then see how *you're* feeling and what *you're* thinking as a participant in that Bible story. Finally, ask yourself what God was saying then and what is God saying to you *now*.' "

"When I tried it," Cliff continued, "the Bible suddenly came to life; and I found I could trust God with anything."

Dear Lord, come into my life and fill me with your presence. I want to trust you with my whole heart. Amen.

JUNE 21
GIVE TO THOSE IN NEED

Do not withhold good from those who deserve it, when it is in your power to act. Do not say to your neighbor, "Come back later; I'll give it tomorrow"—when you now have it with you. —Proverbs 3:27-28

Karen had never seen a real refugee until she met Illie. Illie came to America from Kosovo. She lost her family tragically because of ethnic cleansing. Illie had escaped with only the clothes on her back. Karen had met Illie at the YMCA that was temporarily housing the refugees. They became friends when Karen shared a cookie with her.

All day, Karen kept remembering Illie's desperate eyes; finally, she decided that she needed to do something. So she called Pastor Thompson and said, "I just met a new friend from Kosovo. I want to help her and everybody else there. Is there anything that our church can do? I have thirty dollars I've been saving, and I'd be willing to be a volunteer."

Karen's concern inspired Pastor Thompson to organize an aid effort from the church.

Dear Lord, help me to constantly realize that I do have the power to do good to others. Give me the courage now to share with people in need. Amen.

JUNE 22
THINK BEFORE YOU ACT

It is not good to have zeal without knowledge, nor to be hasty and miss the way. —Proverbs 19:2

Susie thought she was so smart that before anyone could finish giving her instructions, she'd interrupt and say, "I KNOW!"

One night Susie and her boyfriend, Sylvester, were at his house surfing the net looking for music files. They called themselves *RUSH* because they always downloaded the latest music files before their friends could. Sylvester found a new release. Without waiting to be asked, Susie found a stray floppy disk and popped it into the computer to copy the new music files. *RUSH* had done it again!

When Susie got home, she put the floppy disk into her dad's computer to copy the files. As soon as she did, some strange symbols started floating across the screen. The disk had a virus on it. In her haste, Susie had forgotten her dad's rule: "Always check new disks for viruses *before using them*."

Zeal without knowledge leads to disaster.

Dear Lord, teach me how to slow down long enough to learn the important things in life. Amen.

JUNE 23 — KEEP YOUR SPEECH CLEAN

Put away perversity from your mouth; keep corrupt talk far from your lips.
—*Proverbs 4:24*

The nation was shocked when two teenagers tragically massacred innocent students at another small town high school. A TV newscaster tried to read some of the perpetrators' e-mail messages but finally had to stop because the messages were too filthy. Their minds and hearts had become polluted with perversity and corruption. There's a saying: "As a person thinks, so he or she is."

What do you think about all day? You are part of a generation that has access to all types of information—good and bad—through TV, radio, and the Internet. There's another saying: "Garbage in, garbage out." Without God's consistent influence on your life, it will be too easy to let garbage sneak into your mind and leak out of your mouth. Want to keep perversity and corruption from your mouth? Meditate on God's Word.

Dear Lord, your Word says that wise people meditate on your Word day and night. Teach me how to open my mind to good thoughts and avoid corrupt conversations. Amen.

JUNE 24 — HAVE COMPASSION ON THOSE WHO ARE POOR

Those who mock the poor insult their Maker. —*Proverbs 17:5 (NRSV)*

The church youth group could hardly believe the video. Sam, a fifty-year-old man, and his wife, Millie, rummaged through dumpsters and roadside litter looking for discarded aluminum cans. By the end of the day, they returned to a makeshift cardboard shelter under a bridge. Their daily goal was to scrounge enough cans to buy a little food.

Sam and Millie once had a home and nice jobs until Millie unexpectedly needed a costly surgery. Tragically, Sam's company folded the next month. People don't realize that most Americans are only two paychecks away from being homeless. Under similar circumstances, any of us could become poor.

Jesus was born into a poor family; he understands the pain of poverty. God has blessed so many of us with more than we need. Why not consider ways you can help someone who is struggling today?

Dear God, teach me a new level of compassion for poor people. Amen.

JUNE 25 — AVOID PREJUDGING OTHERS

The one who first states a case seems right, until the other comes and cross-examines. —Proverbs 18:17 (NRSV)

"We'd better do something about them quick! They get all the breaks—welfare, food stamps, jobs, everything. They're all lazy, too. You steer clear of 'em, son."

Rob never had any reason to question his father's opinion about "other people" until he went to an international soccer camp. There he met people from South America, the Caribbean, Europe, and Asia. For a solid week they trained together, ate together, lived together, and played together. After it was over, Rob was actually a little embarrassed. The guys from those other countries were so talented. They spoke two or three different languages and knew so many interesting things.

Rob's new friendships made him wonder how many "other people" his father really knew. Rob began to realize the value in getting to know people before making judgments.

Dear Lord, help me to see all sides of an issue before I form an opinion. Amen.

JUNE 26 — JUST LOVE GOD

I love those who love me, and those who seek me find me. —Proverbs 8:17

I once read a fictional story of a man who traveled halfway around the world to ask a wise man where he could find the meaning of life. After a long pause, the wise man instructed the man to climb atop the tallest mountain in the area—there he would find his answer. With much difficulty, the man completed the climb, but he found absolutely nothing. Frustrated, he returned to question the wise man.

"I did all you asked and have found nothing!" he exclaimed. The wise man answered, "Yes, you have; now you know that the answer is not found in difficult tasks. Find meaning in simple things."

Many people think finding God is a difficult task, but it's actually very simple. Just love God with your whole heart. Start by simply telling the Lord that you love him. You'll find that God has been waiting to hear from you.

Dear Lord, I am looking for you today. Help me to find you through the simple act of loving Jesus Christ and loving others. Amen.

DON'T LEND WHAT YOU CANNOT AFFORD TO LOSE!

To guarantee loans for a stranger brings trouble, but there is safety in refusing to do so. —*Proverbs 11:15 (NRSV)*

"Don't ever lend something if you're not prepared to lose it." Today, Terry understood his uncle's warning.

There was a fantastic concert at the new outdoor theater that everybody wanted to attend. Frankie, one of Terry's "friends," had a car, but he didn't have $50 for a ticket. Every day Frankie kept smooth talking his friends, trying to get them to "lend him the money" until he got paid for doing some odd jobs here and there. "I'll even take you guys to the concert in my car," he promised.

Terry had some extra money he'd been saving to buy some shoes. After hearing Frankie's story, he gave in and loaned him the money. Unfortunately, on the day of the concert, Frankie never showed up to pick up Terry and his date. Terry also never got his $50 back.

Be careful about loaning money that you can't afford to lose.

Dear Lord, teach me how to share money and resources for worthy causes. Amen.

BE HUMBLE

When pride comes, then comes disgrace, but with humility comes wisdom. —*Proverbs 11:2*

I learned something from watching a beautiful bird named John Wesley Peacock who lives at Wesley Woods in Atlanta, Georgia. From a distance, the peacock is an amazing array of vivid colors. When he's in a good mood, John Wesley Peacock will open his astonishing tail feathers into a majestic fan. Up to this point, the peacock is most impressive, but there's a down side to this wondrous bird. When John Wesley Peacock opens his mouth, he emits the most horrendous sound that you can imagine. In the middle of the night, Mr. Peacock's piercing cry knifes its way through the wooden walls of the lodges and startles you out of a sound sleep.

Prideful people often look like impressive peacocks from a distance; but when you examine their lives closely, you discover that their selfish speech irritates others. That's why God encourages us to practice humility.

Dear Lord, I want to be known for my humility. Help me to remove any prideful behavior from my life. Amen.

JUNE 29

ALLOW GOD TO COMFORT YOU

The lamp of the LORD searches the spirit . . . it searches out [the] inmost being. —Proverbs 20:27

Christy loved to sing contemporary Christian music. She seemed to know hundreds of songs. She never realized what a blessing that would turn out to be.

During the summer, Christy started getting depressed. She couldn't find any work, she didn't have a boyfriend, and life seemed so boring. Whenever Christy felt depressed, she'd head to her favorite place to sit in the park. It was there that God did a wonderful thing. Words to a song came to Christy's mind— *Thy word is a lamp unto my feet and a light unto my path.*

Like a flood, more and more songs flowed into her heart. God used the words of these songs as a way of comforting Christy's heart. Soon, the depression began to lift from her troubled heart.

Today, remember that God loves you and wants to enter your heart to soothe those places that hurt.

Dear God, search my heart today, comfort me when I'm discouraged, and soothe me when I ache. I need your loving presence in my life. Amen.

JUNE 30

LISTEN AND LEARN

Give instruction to the wise, and they will become wiser still; teach the righteous and they will gain in learning. —Proverbs 9:9 (NRSV)

Gerald sat next to his cousin Phillip and told him about a conversation he'd had with an old man. Years of manual labor had taken their toll on the old man's arthritic body, but that didn't bother him. What did concern him was what he could have done with his life.

"What did the man want to be?" asked Phillip.

"That's the curious thing," replied Gerald. "He said, 'For years I walked past the public library. I never bothered to talk to people who were smarter than I was. I ignored wisdom all my life. I just worked and tried to find a little fun; but I never found out what I had the potential to be.' Then he said to me, 'Don't waste your life, son. Fill your head with something worthwhile.' "

"So," Gerald continued, "I'm trying to figure out what I should do with my life."

Dear Lord, Proverbs 9:9 tells me that wise people listen to instruction and become wiser. Teach me how to fill my head with wisdom and knowledge that are worthwhile. Amen.

JULY

TEEN
TO
TEEN

**Liz Carter, Thomas Charlton,
Christopher Cropsey,
Tai Gregory**

TEEN TO TEEN

**Liz Carter, Thomas Charlton,
Christopher Cropsey, Tai Gregory**

JULY 1-8 LIZ CARTER

JULY 1 FORGIVENESS

Jesus wept. —*John 11:35*

Although this is the shortest verse in the Bible, it tells us so much more than you might think. It shows us that when Jesus assumed the form of man and came to redeem us from our sins, he poured out his power and became a shell of what he truly was. Jesus felt the same emotions, experienced some of the same temptations, and had the same kind of problems that we do. He knows how difficult it is sometimes for us to maintain self-control.

Jesus came to Earth as the ultimate sacrifice so that our sins could be forgiven. Even if sometimes we are angry at others and lose control, Jesus forgives and forgets. That is the kindest thing anyone can do for another.

Remember to forgive others just as Jesus forgave you, and know when to apologize and ask others to forgive you.

Lord, thank you for forgiving me, and please help me to forgive others. Amen.

JULY 2 CHRIST'S SECOND COMING

*So Christ was sacrificed once to take away the sins of many
people; and he will appear a second time, not to bear sin, but to
bring salvation to those who are waiting for him.* —*Hebrews 9:28*

This verse promises that Christ will descend from heaven once more, but for a different purpose. This time, those who believe in him will be taken with him to eternal life in heaven. Believing in Jesus and having a strong relationship with him will be rewarded once and for all on the day that Jesus comes back.

Jesus loved us so much that he was willing to die for us in order to save us. That is the most amazing act of mercy and love that ever took place. The next time you feel unloved, remember that Christ loves you, has always loved you, and will always love you. His mercy is never ending, and it is always waiting for you. His second coming is a symbol of the love he has for you.

Lord, help me to remember and be thankful for what Christ has done and is yet to do for me. Amen.

JULY 3 — THE GOLDEN RULE

Do to others what you would have them do to you, for this sums up the Law and the Prophets. —*Matthew 7:12*

We call this verse the Golden Rule. Just think about it: If everyone followed the guideline of the Golden Rule, our lives would be a whole lot easier. We should treat others like we want to be treated. Now this doesn't mean that we should expect to be treated like we treat others, because we will always encounter people who dislike and mistreat everyone. But if we act on this verse, we *will* help ourselves and others. Try it today and see what happens!

Lord, help me to follow the Golden Rule. Amen.

JULY 4 — THE NARROW GATE

Enter through the narrow gate. For wide is the gate and broad is the road that leads to destruction, and many enter through it. —*Matthew 7:13*

This passage tells us that we should always walk the path of God's will, even if sometimes it seems hard.

Have you ever been pressured to insult others to gain popularity, or to cheat? I know from my own experience that doing what is right is seldom easy—and the path that *seems* easy often ends up being incredibly hard. Say that you are in a crowd of popular people who are insulting someone. A really good put-down comes to your mind, and you say it. Most likely, the person will eventually hear that comment and be embarrassed and resentful. What seemed easy at the time ends up being a big mess.

A sheep won't charge off a cliff, but gradually it may gnaw at the grass just a little bit closer to the cliff until, before you know it, thud! That's the way it is with morality. It deteriorates very gradually. We keep that from happening by always walking with God.

Lord, help me to walk the narrow path of righteousness with you. Amen.

JULY 5 TEMPTATION

Blessed is anyone who endures temptation. Such a one has stood the test and will receive the crown of life that the Lord has promised to those who love him. —James 1:12 (NRSV)

This passage tells us that God wants us to *endure* temptation. What does that mean?

When I was younger, I used to read in church all the time. One day my mother took my book away from me, and I was furious. Throughout the sermon, I was fuming; but after church, I decided not to express my anger. My mother saw my self-control, and later she took me to my favorite bookstore!

This analogy may be a stretch, but it communicates the general idea. If you can show self-control, a willingness to serve God and sacrifice for God, and faithfulness to God no matter what the cost, you will be rewarded.

I know it's not easy. Resisting temptation, especially when you are mad, is just about the hardest thing in the world. But remember: "With God all things are possible" (Matthew 19:26).

Lord, please help me to resist temptation today. Amen.

JULY 6 ARE YOU LUKEWARM?

So, because you are lukewarm—neither hot nor cold—I am about to spit you out of my mouth. —Revelation 3:16

Are you "lukewarm"? Think of it this way: "all-out Christians" are "hot," unbelievers are "cold," and those who say they are Christians but don't really know the Lord are "lukewarm." The surprising thing is that being "lukewarm" is even worse than being "cold."

Even those who truly believe in God can be "lukewarm" by letting other things have a higher priority than their relationship with God and by keeping their faith to themselves. We can't "sit in the back" and do just enough to "get by"; God wants our total commitment.

A song many of us learned as little kids says it all: "This little light of mine, I'm gonna let it shine." We must let our light shine—let our faith be visible to others—and never hide it.

Help me to shine my light, Lord, so that others may see you in me. Amen.

JULY 7 REACH OUT

Jesus answered, "I am the way and the truth and the life. No one comes to the Father except through me." —*John 14:6*

This verse tells us that no one gets to the Father except through the Son. That means believing in Jesus Christ is the only way to receive eternal life—to get into heaven. Many people use this verse when they evangelize others, telling them that if they don't believe in Jesus, they'll go to hell. But God doesn't want us to frighten others into believing in Christ. We aren't Christians out of fear, but out of love.

Jesus wants us to reach out and share his love so that others may come to know him. He wants everyone to know the way to everlasting life and peace. He wants us to share the good news with others.

Society has branded this a cruel, intolerant verse, but that just isn't true. Jesus isn't intolerant; only people are. Reach out and share his all-inclusive love.

Lord, help me reach out to others, share your love, and help them follow you. Amen.

JULY 8 AFRAID OF DYING?

It is better to go to a house of mourning than to go to a house of feasting, for death is the destiny of [everyone]; the living should take this to heart. —*Ecclesiastes 7:2*

A recent poll indicated that one of the greatest fears of Americans is death. Interestingly, other polls have shown that 96 percent of Americans believe in God. I don't know how many of this 96 percent are *Christians,* but I imagine it's a pretty good number—which is why I have a hard time reconciling these two polls. Those who truly believe that Jesus saves should not fear death, for their souls are safe. Their present bodies are only the "packaging."

As today's verse says, the destiny of every person on this Earth is to eventually die. But life doesn't end with death. Those who believe in Jesus Christ are promised eternal life with him. Although death is sad for those who have lost a loved one, we must remember that it is a wonderful beginning—not an ending.

Lord, help me not to fear death; help me to understand that it is not an ending but a beginning. Amen.

JULY 9-16 THOMAS CHARLTON

 # JULY 9 — SHOW YOUR FAITH

Don't let anyone look down on you because you are young, but set an example for the believers in speech, in life, in love, in faith and in purity. —1 Timothy 4:12

Back when I was in junior high, I played golf with my friends all the time during the summer. We loved to play, but the older men always complained about us taking up the course. Those men did not respect our playing ability because we were young. One day a friend and I went to the course to play. When we arrived, two of those older men did not have partners, and they needed us to complete a foursome. After we played with them, the men realized that we were not as bad as they had thought. After that, they never complained about us again.

It's the same way in our Christian walk: In order to get older Christians to respect our walk, we must show them our faith and our love of Christ.

Dear Father, do not let anyone look down on me because I am young. Help me make others believers through my speech, my life, my love, and my faith in you. Amen.

 # JULY 10 — REVENGE

Do not repay anyone evil for evil. —Romans 12:17

One summer I was at my girlfriend's house when her little brother came to tell me that my car had just been rolled with toilet paper. I was infuriated to see my car completely covered in white toilet paper. Then, all of a sudden, I saw my twin brother drive by and wave at me. My first thought was to get revenge. So the next day, a couple of friends and I went to the grocery store and bought toilet paper, marshmallow cream, clam juice, flour, and sardines. We then proceeded to trash my brother's Honda Accord. The following day, when the sun hit the car, it literally baked the substances on the car and completely ruined the paint job.

My father decided that I had gone over the line, and I was punished. The fact that I was punished but my brother wasn't upset me greatly. Even though I was upset, I realized that revenge only hurts one person, and that's the person seeking it. The Bible tells us not to repay anyone evil for evil because we will only hurt ourselves and those around us. Revenge never makes any situation better.

Dear God, help me not to seek revenge but to love those who have wronged me. Amen.

 # EVIL DESIRES

Flee the evil desires of youth, and pursue righteousness, faith, love and peace, along with those who call on the Lord out of a pure heart.
—2 Timothy 2:22

One of the major problems for Christian teens is the everyday worldly temptations we face. It is extremely hard to stay away from these temptations all the time. The world tells us that these evil desires, such as drugs and sex, are okay; but the Bible tells us that they are not. There is only one way to get the strength to stay away from these things, and that is through Jesus Christ, our Lord and Savior. If we pray and pursue righteousness, then we can go to the Lord with a pure heart. It is so easy to give in to temptation. When you do fall down, then your relationship with God becomes distant. Don't let that happen; hold on to the strength you can receive through prayer.

Dear Lord, help me to resist evil desires, and give me the strength to do this through prayer with you. Amen.

 # WALK THE WALK

Do not merely listen to the word, and so deceive yourselves. Do what it says.
—James 1:22

You've probably heard the phrase, "If you are going to talk the talk, then you must walk the walk." This phrase couldn't be more right. Don't just read the Word and then ignore it; read the Word and live it. One of the biggest turn-offs to those who do not know God are people who claim they do and then don't show it in their actions. Carry the love of God with you always, and show it in your deeds.

Dear Father, help me to walk the walk that you have for me. Help me not to be a hypocrite but to put my faith into practice. Amen.

JULY 13 | HOPE

My dear children, I write this to you so that you will not sin. But if anybody does sin, we have one who speaks to the Father in our defense—Jesus Christ, the Righteous One. He is the atoning sacrifice for our sins, and not only for ours but also for the sins of the whole world. —1 John 2:1-2

We have all sinned and strayed away from the righteous path that God has set for us. The good news is that even though we do sin, that is not the end of the story. The Lord sent his only Son to die for us on the cross so that we can renew ourselves and be righteous. Christ is on our side and is our defense against sin and all that is wicked. Through Christ, we can ask forgiveness. He gives us great hope for fighting another day.

Dear God, help me to know that even when I fall, I can still come to you for forgiveness. Amen.

JULY 14 | PERSEVERANCE

I have fought the good fight, I have finished the race, I have kept the faith. —2 Timothy 4:7

When I was a little kid, everyone on my street played football in my front yard every day after school. The teams were always about even, and so this made scoring a touchdown a big deal. All of us boys, and even some girls, would beat on one another during the game. Because of this physical contact, someone would always get hurt and run home crying; and that is how the game would end. When someone finally did score, it was such a big deal that all the pain from the beatings went away. This is just like the reward that God has for us because of the race we have run. Any pain that we have had will be overshadowed by the paradise we call heaven.

Dear God, help me to run the race you have set for me, and remind me that the reward is greater than anything the world has to offer. Amen.

JULY 15 ANGER

"In your anger do not sin": Do not let the sun go down while you are still angry.
　　　　　　　　　　　　　　　　　　　　　　—Ephesians 4:26

Most of us get angry easily. We let our tempers get away from us, and we wind up hurting our relationships with family and friends. We all do this from time to time. When we get angry, often we do not think about the consequences of our anger-filled actions.

I have heard tragic stories about teenagers who got terribly mad at one of their parents over something insignificant, and then, before they could apologize, the parent died suddenly and unexpectedly. Do not let this happen to you. In the Bible it tells us not to go to bed while we are still angry at someone, because we might not have a chance to say we're sorry. Anger is something from the world, and nothing good can come from it.

Dear Heavenly Father, please do not let anger fill our hearts and ruin relationships with those we love. Amen.

JULY 16 DEATH IS NOT THE END

You will not abandon me to the grave, nor will you let your Holy One see decay.
　　　　　　　　　　　　　　　　　　　　　　—Psalm 16:10

The summer after my sophomore year in high school, one of my friend's mother was diagnosed with cancer. The cancer was so bad that the doctors said she was beyond recovery. Healing services were held for her, as well as private prayer meetings, in hopes that God would give her a miracle and heal her. It turned out that it was not the Lord's will. She died in the middle of that summer.

Then came the slow process of healing the wounds of friends and family who were grieving. Some people were mad at God because of this woman's untimely death, but perhaps they did not understand that the Lord never abandons us. Because of Christ Jesus, our Savior, this woman is now in paradise.

When people die, it is important for us to know and remember that this is not the end. Because of our faith as Christians, we all will be reunited in the kingdom of heaven. There always will be a period of mourning after someone dies, but we can find reassurance in the grace that God gives us because of his son Jesus Christ's death on the cross.

Dear God, help us to know and remember that when someone close to us dies, you will not abandon them—or us. Amen.

GOD LOVES YOU

For I am convinced that neither death nor life, neither angels nor demons, neither the present nor the future, nor any powers, neither height nor depth, nor anything else in all creation, will be able to separate us from the love of God that is in Christ Jesus our Lord.

—*Romans 8:38-39*

Wow! It's incredible to think that big ol' God loves little us, but it's true. And even better than that, God loves us so much that nothing can separate us from him. It's wonderful to think that even when it seems everyone else has abandoned you, God is still right there, loving you. It's completely mind boggling, because no one on earth can offer the unconditional love that God does. In spite of our shortcomings, God loves us anyway, and that's what being a Christian is all about.

Thank you so much for your unconditional love, Lord. Help me to always be aware of it. Amen.

GOD CAN USE YOU

Don't let anyone look down on you because you are young, but set an example for the believers in speech, in life, in love, in faith and in purity. —*1 Timothy 4:12*

One of the greatest thoughts we can have as Christians is that the God of the universe, the God who created everything and watches over it, can use us to make a difference. It is extremely simple to use our age as an excuse for not getting up and doing something for God. However, God leaves us no loophole. It is plain that God wants us to change this world.

God also tells us exactly how to bring about this change: by setting an example. As Christians, we must make a difference by living what we believe. Our peers are watching us to see if we are genuine; and when we prove to them that we are, the impact will be incredible.

Lord, thank you for allowing me to be used by you. Help me serve you by being an example to others. Amen.

JULY 19 — GOD HAS A PLAN FOR YOU

"For I know the plans I have for you," declares the LORD, "plans to prosper you and not to harm you, plans to give you hope and a future."
—Jeremiah 29:11

As young Christians, one of our greatest blessings and most exciting thoughts is that God has a special plan for our lives. Each and every one of us has a future that God has mapped out ahead of time. The fact that God has a blueprint for each of us is exciting enough, but it's even greater to think that God wants to "prosper" us! Here is God, all-powerful, and his plan for my life and yours is for us to be blessed.

It's not a free ride, though. We have to hold up our end of the bargain: following him. We can't grow into God's future for us unless we consciously serve him. And when we do, we have the joy of knowing that we will have a wonderful future.

God, thank you for the plan you have for my life. Help me to live for you and to be obedient to your will for my life. Amen.

JULY 20 — WHO IS YOUR "IDEAL"?

To this you were called, because Christ suffered for you, leaving you an example, that you should follow in his steps.
—1 Peter 2:21

Has there ever been anyone in your life who was your "ideal"? By *ideal*, I mean someone you want to be more like. It could be a movie star, a sports figure, or maybe a parent or someone at school. It's funny the things we do to imitate this person. Sadly, sometimes we do negative things to be like our ideal.

Who could be a better ideal than Christ Jesus? He was sinless; he lived a perfect life. He sacrificed himself for us. He was the Son of God. Now those are lofty goals to live up to, but as the saying goes, "If you aim for nothing, you'll hit it every time." Make Jesus your ideal, and you will find joy and peace in your life.

Lord Jesus, help me make you my ideal. Empower me to follow the example you set for me. Amen.

JULY 21 "I'M NOT GOOD ENOUGH"

"But Lord," Gideon asked, "how can I save Israel? My clan is the weakest in Manasseh, and I am the least in my family."
—Judges 6:15

We all have days when we feel like Gideon did—days when we feel like everyone is better than us. Sometimes it may be true; sometimes it may be only our perception. But in either case, it is a dangerous feeling. This line of thought can lead to self-hatred, to isolation, and in some cases, to suicide. So how can we avoid this problem?

One of the best things to do is to avoid comparing yourself to those around you. In this verse, Gideon demonstrates the problem. He weighed himself against those around him and said that he was weak. But God called Gideon to look to him for Gideon's worth—and God calls us to do the same today. God gave me specific traits, and he gave me those traits for a purpose. The more I focus on trying to be like someone else instead of focusing on God, the worse I feel.

Make God your focus, and you will realize just how "wonderfully made" you are (Psalm 139:14).

God, help me to avoid comparing myself to others. Let me feel worthy as your child. Amen.

JULY 22 TRIAL BY FIRE

Consider it pure joy . . . whenever you face trials of many kinds.
—James 1:2

This is one of those verses that sounds wonderful most of the time. As long as everything in life is going fine, we love to quote it. But when trials do come, suddenly this verse vanishes from our memory. Who could actually be happy during the hard times anyway? I certainly don't love being tested.

The answer is found in the difference between happiness and joy. Happiness is a feeling that changes constantly and is based on your current condition, whereas joy is an emotion based on a future hope and does not change frequently. Notice that God doesn't call us to be happy about being tried. Instead, God asks us to have the positive outlook that we are becoming more like him. If we accomplish this, the trials themselves may not be easier, but at least we will have assurance that our pain is not worthless.

God, when trials come, help me to be joyful as I focus on becoming more like you. Amen.

JULY 23 RUNNING THE RACE

Do you not know that in a race all the runners run, but only one gets the prize? Run in such a way as to get the prize.
—*1 Corinthians 9:24*

As young Christians, this verse inspires us because we still have a long way to run in our race. One of the important things to remember about this verse is that how you begin the race is not what gets you the prize. In many races, the person who begins in first place does not win in the end. It is how you finish the race that wins you the prize. If you are running in a mile race, you'll never win by running really fast only at the beginning and end. You have to be consistent throughout the race. That is exactly how God wants us to live our lives. God doesn't want us to be strong in him only when we first become Christians and then, again, when we die. He wants us to run hard the whole time. Only then will we receive the ultimate prize.

Lord, help me run hard in the race of life. Only with your help will I be able to finish in such a way that I may receive the prize. Amen.

JULY 24 FRIENDS

A friend loves at all times, and kinsfolk are born to share adversity.
—*Proverbs 17:17 (NRSV)*

Life would be very difficult for us without friends. God has designed us as social beings, and we desire the comfort and enjoyment we get from having bonds with other humans. Among those bonds, the ones we share with good friends are some of the most meaningful.

God gives us advice and instruction to help us with our friendships. He doesn't want us to give up on friends when we go through rough times. Instead, we are to love "at all times." God wants us to love our friends with the kind of love that desires the best for them. And above all, God wants us to encourage one another so that we can reach our ultimate goal: to be like him.

God, thank you so much for the friends you have placed in my life. Help me to be the kind of friend they need. Amen.

JULY 25 UNDERSTANDING

Great is our Lord and mighty in power; his understanding has no limit. —Psalm 147:5

Sometimes life doesn't make sense, and we have a hard time understanding why things have to be the way they are. But, in time, we learn that there are some things we'll never understand, and that's okay. God just asks us to trust him. He wants us to know that no matter what happens in our lives, he will always be there for us. God will always offer us a shoulder to cry on and an ear that is willing to listen when we are ready to talk. Every time you pray, remember that God hears you—and he understands.

God, grant me the ability to understand things I don't want to understand—and the patience that comes "along the way." Amen.

JULY 26 LET GO AND LET GOD

Cast all your anxiety on [God] because he cares for you.
—1 Peter 5:7

When we are stressed out and having a really bad day, we often seem to let go of the most important and awesome thing in our lives: God. What happens is, we put God on the back burner and worry about our problems ourselves. Instead of "letting go and letting God," we let God go completely. From now on, when you find yourself in a situation that you just can't handle, let it go and let God deal with it.

God, give me the faith to give you my problems—especially when they are too great for me to handle. Amen.

JULY 27 PARENTS

Children, obey your parents in the Lord, for this is right. "Honor your father and mother"—which is the first commandment with a promise—"that it may go well with you and that you may enjoy long life on the earth." —Ephesians 6:1-3

147

Whether we like to admit it or not, our parents are a little like God. True, they're far from perfect, but think about it: They provide a safe place for us to live, they give us food when we are hungry, they take care of us when we are sick, and they love us—even when we really don't deserve it. Doesn't God do the same? He protects us, he meets all our physical needs and gives us his knowledge when we are hungry for it, he is there for us when we need healing, and he loves us through thick and thin.

Just as we should respect God, we also should respect our parents. Take a minute today to let your parents—or whoever is a parent figure in your life—know how much they mean to you. Thank them for everything they've done for you. Then thank God for letting them be there for you— just as he will always be there for you.

Thank you, Lord, for the gift of parents and others who show us how much you love us. Thank you for letting us know that you will always be there for us. Amen.

JULY 28 — HEAVEN AND HELL

Then the King will say to those on his right, "Come, you who are blessed by my Father; take your inheritance, the kingdom prepared for you since the creation of the world." Then he will say to those on his left, "Depart from me, you who are cursed, into the eternal fire prepared for the devil and his angels." —Matthew 25:34, 41

Take a minute and imagine everyone and everything you love—whether they are concrete or abstract, real or unreal. Now, imagine that in one second, all of it is taken from you; you can no longer have or see the people and things you love ever again.

Just as it was easy for you to imagine the people and things you love, it's probably easy for you to imagine heaven. Don't you think it's a perfect place full of love? And just as it was hard for you to imagine life without the people and things you love, it's probably hard for you to imagine hell. Why is that? For many of us, maybe it's because we wonder why we should imagine a hell when we can choose something as great as heaven. But the Bible reminds us that both heaven and hell are real. Where we will spend eternity is a personal decision. Just remember how much better it is to have love.

Lord, thank you for giving me the choice to one day be with you in heaven. Amen.

THE WORD

All scripture is inspired by God and is useful for teaching, for reproof, for correction, and for training in righteousness, so that everyone who belongs to God may be proficient, equipped for every good work. —*2 Timothy 3:16-17 (NRSV)*

There is this awesome book given to us directly from God. It starts off by telling us how everything was made, and by the end, we know about many things—from faith, hope, and love to how Christ died for us to wash away our sins. It always seems to hold all the answers to what's going on in our lives. You see, you can always turn to the Word—whether you're up or down, excited or depressed. When you read the Word, you gain something besides the wisdom of the Scriptures—you gain God.

Lord, remind me to turn to your Word when I am happy or sad, when I'm feeling afraid or lonely, or when I just need some assurance. Amen.

AFRAID OF WITNESSING

Therefore go and make disciples of all nations, baptizing them in the name of the Father and of the Son and of the Holy Spirit, and teaching them to obey everything I have commanded you. And surely I am with you always, to the very end of the age. —*Matthew 28:19-20*

So many times in a single day we are given the chance to share the love of God, but often we are so afraid of what others may think that we put it aside. We let our thoughts get in the way of actions that could possibly save a life for Christ. Sometimes we just have to break out of our shell and let others know the greatness of God. Witnessing can be a smile that lets others know someone cares, or it may be actually sitting down and telling others about the gospel story. When given the chance, let others know that someone cares. Share the love of Christ today with someone who really needs him.

Awesome God, help me to proclaim and worship your name in everything I say and do—without fear. Amen.

SPREAD THE LOVE

A new command I give you: Love one another. As I have loved you, so you must love one another. —John 13:34

Is it hard for you to spread the love of Christ? For some people, the only time they hear of the love of Christ is when others share it. The love of Christ is so huge and so strong, there's enough for anyone who wants it. It's free, and it's everlasting. All Christ asks in return is that we spread his love to others who need it. Just by spreading the love, we gain greater things: faith, hope, love, and everlasting life.

God, give me the will to share and spread your love in Christ. Amen.

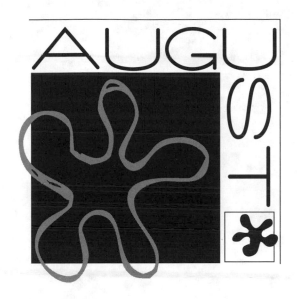

CARING
FOR
ONE
ANOTHER

Clare Golson Doyle

CARING FOR ONE ANOTHER

Clare Golson Doyle

FOLLOW THE GREATEST COMMANDMENT

Jesus replied: " 'Love the Lord your God with all your heart and with all your soul and with all your mind.' This is the first and greatest commandment. And the second is like it: 'Love your neighbor as yourself.' " —Matthew 22:37-39

What a commandment! That is all God calls us to do: to love God and to love our neighbors. The two go hand in hand, because one of the best ways we show our love for God is by loving our neighbors. But how do we do this?

Loving our neighbors means we have to be concerned about others. We have to do more than take a casual interest in them; we have to care *about* them and *for* them. Caring is not always easy, but that is what God wants us to do.

In the days ahead we will spend time looking at what the Bible says to us about caring for our neighbors. I invite you to look at your world—and your neighbors—and begin to take seriously the commandment you have been given.

Dear God, help me to follow your commandment to love my neighbors as myself. Amen.

IMITATE GOD'S LOVE

Be imitators of God, therefore, as dearly loved children and live a life of love, just as Christ loved us and gave himself up for us as a fragrant offering and sacrifice to God. —Ephesians 5:1-2

As I was writing these devotions, I was talking with a friend about what teens deal with and how it feels to be a teen. He said, "It's scary." He was exactly right. As a teen, you are no longer a child, but you are not yet an adult. Your body is changing rapidly, and you are experiencing many pressures. It is indeed a scary time.

As a Christian, you have an advantage. You have your faith, and you have Christian friends who are there for you. This is why it is so important for us to care for one another—so that we may help one another through the difficult, scary times of life. We must be imitators of God, trying to live a life of love just as Jesus did.

Dear God, thank you for loving me so much that you gave up your Son. Help me to imitate you and to love others. Amen.

LOVE ONE ANOTHER

Let no debt remain outstanding, except the continuing debt to love one another, for [one] who loves [others] has fulfilled the law. . . . And whatever other commandment there may be, are summed up in this one rule: "Love your neighbor as yourself."
—*Romans 13:8, 9b*

I was a PK. That's right, a preacher's kid. Because Dad was appointed to a different church every few years and we would have to move, my sisters and I had to change schools a lot. Yet everywhere we went, there was always at least one kid our age who helped us to settle in, learn the school, and understand what was supposed to happen when and where. These young people were a great help to us. They helped us to know what was going on and what was expected. They helped us to make a place for ourselves in our new "homes." They made a real difference in our lives by living out Jesus' command to love one another.

Dear God, help me to live out Jesus' command to love one another, and help me to reach out to someone new. Amen.

USE YOUR GIFTS

Each one should use whatever gift he [or she] has received to serve others, faithfully administering God's grace in its various forms.
—*1 Peter 4:10*

When I was growing up, I was always "stuck" with the task of organization. "Clare, organize this"; "Clare, organize that." It happened at home; it happened at school; it happened at church. Why did I always have to do all the work? Why did I have to plan and arrange and get things going?

Why? Because I'm good at it. I like things to be organized and in the right place. I like things to go smoothly. I like making things happen. God has given me this gift, and I can use it to serve others.

Today, think about your gifts. What can you do well? Then choose one of your gifts and think of a way you can use it to serve others this week. God has made you very special, and God can use you to share grace with others.

Dear God, help me use the gifts you have given me so that I may serve others. Amen.

LOVE DEEPLY AND FORGIVE FREELY

Above all, love each other deeply, because love covers over a multitude of sins.　　　　　　　　　　　　　*—1 Peter 4:8*

For several summers I participated in an exciting morning devotion where we would go to an amphitheater on the lakeshore early in the morning and watch a reenactment of Jesus' appearance to the disciples after his resurrection. During this reenactment, I saw over and over how Jesus called on Peter to feed his sheep. And I remembered how Jesus called Peter "the rock." Peter was the rock upon which the church was founded.

Peter was not perfect. He was impatient. He missed out on important ideas. He was a sinner. He even denied Jesus three times before the crucifixion. But Jesus saw the good in Peter. He saw what potential Peter had. And most important, Jesus loved Peter and forgave him for his failures. Jesus expects us to do the same thing with our brothers and sisters.

Dear God, help me to love as freely as Jesus did. Help me to forgive those who do wrong to me. Amen.

ENCOURAGE OTHERS

Therefore encourage one another and build each other up, just as in fact you are doing.　　　　　　　*—1 Thessalonians 5:11*

Year after year after year, Mary tried. She tried to pass the physical fitness exam at school. It was a goal. It was a good goal. And every year she got a little better—but not much. Oh, she could run the laps and jump far enough. She could do the jumping jacks and sit-ups. But, heaven help her, she could not support her weight on the chin-up bar. It was torture. Every year she failed at this part of the test.

Then one day she met Janet. They became good friends, and finally Mary confided to Janet her fear of taking the test again. The test was to take place in April. In January, Janet started encouraging Mary. She told Mary every day that she thought this would be the year Mary would pass. She helped Mary practice day after day after day. She timed her with a stopwatch at practice each day until, one day, Mary started to meet the required time limit of ten seconds on the chin-up bar. Finally Mary thought, *Maybe I can do this*. And she did! She passed the exam.

Dear God, thank you for friends who encourage me and build me up. Help me to encourage and build up others. Amen.

# REJOICE WITH OTHERS

Let us not become conceited, provoking and envying each other.
—Galatians 5:26

My friends and I were seated in the gym with the rest of the school. The awards had just been given out, and our friend had been named valedictorian of the senior class. We all were happy for her. The guys in front of us were talking about our sophomore class, looking to the future and debating which of them would be the head of our class. They were sure it would be one of the three of them. They never mentioned anyone else, including me. *How conceited of them!* I thought. I was jealous of them. I wanted to be included. Would I ever be part of their group? Did I really want to be part of their group, or did I just want to be better than they were?

Dear God, help me not to think I am better than other people, and help me not to envy what others have. Instead, O God, help me to grow and rejoice with others. Amen.

# DON'T BE A GRUMBLER

Don't grumble against each other . . . or you will be judged. The Judge is standing at the door!
—James 5:9

She was my best friend—that is, until she started getting everything I didn't get. It was a terrific time for her, but it was a miserable time for me. She made the school publicity team; I didn't. She made the school choir; I didn't—for the second time. She got a fabulous part-time job with flexible hours; I got a difficult part-time job with no flexibility. She seemed to have it all. It was so unfair. It just wasn't right. Why did she get everything while I got nothing? It was a hard time, and it began to affect our friendship. I grumbled a good bit.

Then one day, in the midst of all my grumbling, I finally realized that I was doing exactly what the Bible said I should not do. Instead of grumbling, I should have been supporting her, rejoicing with her, and realizing that things for me were not so bad. I didn't want to be judged by God as a grumbler. I had to change my ways.

Dear God, sometimes it is hard not to grumble against others. Please help me to love them and not grumble enviously against them. Amen.

WASH ANOTHER'S FEET

Now that I, your Lord and Teacher, have washed your feet, you also should wash one another's feet. —John 13:14

Washing one another's feet: How can we do that? On a spiritual level, we can do it by taking care of one another, by serving one another. There are all kinds of ways to serve others.

When I was a junior in high school, my class was responsible for planning the senior prom. For months and months, I helped plan for the big night. As the weekend of the dance approached, it became obvious that I was not going to have a date. I was miserable, lonely, and mostly embarrassed. I decided the best thing was to leave town and visit my grandparents. I told my friend Anna what I was going to do. She asked to come with me, and we had a fabulous time. My grandparents treated us like royalty and really spoiled us. Anna did not have to go; she had plenty of opportunities for the weekend. But she chose to be with me and help me through a difficult time. In a way, she "washed my feet" that weekend.

Dear God, help me learn how to "wash another's feet" in whatever way they may need. Amen.

BE KIND AND COMPASSIONATE

Be kind and compassionate to one another, forgiving each other, just as in Christ God forgave you. —Ephesians 4:32

There were about six in the group—sometimes more. They were great friends and had so much in common. They liked school, they were in the band together, they were good students, and they went to the same church. They did not date a lot, they did not drink, they did not do drugs, and they did not "fool around" with boys. They were "good girls." A lot of the other kids at school made fun of them, calling them "girl scouts." Instead of being offended, the girls were honored; they adopted the nickname and became proud of it. They forgave those who made fun of them because they knew that was what God wanted them to do—because they knew that because of their example, others might learn to be kind and compassionate, too.

Dear God, help me to be kind to others today as you want me to be. Amen.

TRY TO GET ALONG

If you keep on biting and devouring each other, watch out or you will be destroyed by each other. —Galatians 5:15

It was spring; graduation was just days away. We were excited. Twelve years of preparation and waiting were finally about to pay off. And then it happened: *the fight.* It was racial. Our school was ethnically mixed, and 99 percent of the time everybody got along. But something went wrong. The girls, one from each ethnic group, kept picking at one another until . . . *the fight.* They came to blows, and it was ugly. The school, unfortunately, split down ethnic lines, and the tension was tremendous. The principal announced that graduation might be canceled. *Canceled?* We were devastated. How could this be?

Isn't that what Paul is talking about here in Galatians? Our inability to get along can destroy us and the things around us. Our graduation was about to be destroyed because we could not get along. Things finally settled down enough that we were able to have our graduation ceremony, but what should have been a joyous evening was an evening filled with tension.

Dear God, help me to get along with others so that we can build friendships and not destroy one another. Amen.

CARRY EACH OTHER'S BURDENS

Carry each other's burdens, and in this way you will fulfill the law of Christ. —Galatians 6:2

Carla was really down. What would she do now? Her grandmother had been so special to her, and now Carla had to go on without her.

Carla sat at the funeral home with her family, waiting to greet all the visitors who would come. How would she get through the evening? It seemed hopelessly impossible. At five minutes until five, the doors were opened for the visitation to begin. Minutes later, in came most of the youth group from Carla's church. They sat with her and talked with her the entire visitation time. They did not leave.

Carla's burden had been shared. Her youth group had seen her through the evening.

Dear God, at times my life can be so hard and my burdens can be so heavy. Thank you for Christian friends who help to carry me through. Amen.

LIVE IN HARMONY

Live in harmony with one another.　　　　　—Romans 12:16a

When I was young, I visited a kibbutz in Northern Israel. The people there lived in community. They shared everything and lived in harmony. Each person had a primary responsibility for the life of the community, and they lived peaceably together. This was a unique place, but it was so foreign to me and my traveling companions.

Our society is competitive and self-centered. Most of the time, we are more interested in ourselves than in others. And we really are not concerned about getting along with anybody unless that person can do something for us. But God calls us to live in harmony with all of our brothers and sisters.

What can you do to live in harmony with others?

Dear God, help me to live in harmony with those around me. Amen.

LOVE EVERYONE

My command is this: Love each other as I have loved you.
　　　　　　　　　　　　　　　　　　　　—John 15:12

She was in my youth group, and she bugged me a lot. She really got on my nerves. In fact, I did not like her at all. She was pretty, intelligent, and liked by everybody—except me. I did not understand it. Then one day our youth group had a program on this scripture from John, and I understood. I did not have to like her, but I did have to love her. Jesus did not give us any leeway. He did not say, "Love each other if you like each other." He simply said, "Love each other." I realized that this means everybody, even the girl who was always talking with *my* friends and getting on my nerves.

Dear God, help me to love other people—even the ones I don't like. Amen.

BEAR WITH ONE ANOTHER

Be completely humble and gentle; be patient, bearing with one another in love. —Ephesians 4:2

He was different and so smart. It was obvious he was not part of the "in crowd." She wasn't either, but she sure was trying to be. Most of their classmates made fun of him or ignored him.

School had not been in session long when he started to pay attention to her. At first she was shocked, frustrated, and even angry; then she realized that it was a compliment and an honor. There was no way she ever would have considered dating him; but at the same time, she did not want to hurt him. Should she lead him on, or should she ignore him? Instead of choosing either, she decided to be honest with him. She thanked him for his interest, told him that she did not want to date, and suggested that they could be friends. They did become friends—good friends. In fact, their friendship has lasted beyond high school for many, many years.

As Christians, we are called to be gentle with each other, always concerned about the other person's feelings.

Dear God, help me to be kind in all of my relationships. May others see Christ in the way that I treat them. Amen.

EXCLUDE NO ONE

We put no stumbling block in anyone's path, so that our ministry will not be discredited. —2 Corinthians 6:3

She wanted to fit in. She came every week to everything the church offered. But it seemed she always wound up sitting alone. She must have been terribly lonely. She was getting something out of church, but something was missing. Adults would give her a cursory hello, the children just ignored her, and the youth group tolerated her but basically had nothing to do with her. Then she started bringing a friend. At least she had company, but still the two were left alone. Gradually, they dropped out of the weekly youth meeting until, one day, they just never came back. She was a person seeking God, wanting to be part of God's kingdom, and yet the people of the church excluded her. They became a stumbling block to her faith.

Consider your own church, your own youth group. Do you help others to feel welcome? Do you include new people in your group?

Dear God, help me to be more open to others, and help me not to be a stumbling block to anyone. Amen.

AUGUST 17 — LOVE AS JESUS LOVED

A new command I give you: Love one another. As I have loved you, so you must love one another. By this all men will know that you are my disciples, if you love one another. —John 13:34-35

Loving one another means loving those we like and those we don't like; those who are like us and those who are different from us; those who have no problems and those who have many problems. My best friend's youth group had a great way of showing love to others that demonstrated they were truly disciples of Jesus. Every year they would work a long time to prepare a party for a group of disabled children. At the party they would play games, serve refreshments, and give the children special presents they had made. It was a great party, and everybody always had a good time. This youth group truly showed what it means to love one another.

Dear God, what can I do today to make a difference in some-one's life? What can I do so that others will know I am a disciple of your Son, Jesus Christ? Amen.

AUGUST 18 — BE TRUTHFUL

Do not lie to each other, since you have taken off your old self with its practices and have put on the new self, which is being renewed in knowledge in the image of its Creator. —Colossians 3:9-10

Our culture tells us it is all right to lie. Every day we see evidence suggesting that lying is OK. Politicians do it. Advertisers do it. Businesses do it. *Everybody* does it, don't they?

Our culture may tell us that lying is OK, but the Bible tells us clearly that it is not acceptable. As Christians, we have put away our sinfulness and become new creatures in Christ. We have a new way to act and behave. That means we must not lie. We must be honest with one another—not deceitful. Jesus calls us to live in his image and, therefore, we must not lie to our brothers and sisters.

Dear God, help me to live in your image, being truthful in all my relationships. Amen.

CONFESS YOUR SINS

Therefore confess your sins to each other and pray for each other so that you may be healed. —James 5:16a

Confess your sins to each other. Yeah, right! Actually, it *does* make a difference.

I took an advanced math class as a sophomore. We always broke for lunch in the middle of class. One day we were taking a difficult test, and I was confused about one of the rules I needed to know. If I could just remember the rule correctly, I could solve the problem. I knew the rule went one of two ways. I wouldn't really be cheating if I asked about the rule at lunch, would I? Well, I asked, I solved the problem, and I made a 100 on the test. Hurrah for me, right? Wrong! I was miserable. I could not eat. I could not sleep. I could not concentrate on anything. Finally, I realized that I would have to confess. I confessed to my friends and to my teacher. As soon as I confessed, I began to feel better. I began to be healed.

My "punishment" was different than might be expected. The entire class got a lecture on cheating. Everybody knew I was the one who "blew the whistle" on our lunch discussion. Even though they were angry with me, I was still glad that my conscience was clear and that I was not living a lie.

Dear God, I am a sinner, and I make mistakes. Help me to confess so that I may be healed. Amen.

LOVE THOSE WHO ARE DIFFERENT

Love one another deeply, from the heart. —1 Peter 1:22b

These kids are cool. Even though they are so different and have so little in common, they get along so well. Jake likes jazz. Ellen's a cheerleader. Bob's a great mechanic. Felicia's from South America. Ray's African American. What's the deal?

These kids are in the same youth group at church, and they spend time together. They respect one another and their differences, but more important, they love one another. They do not always have to like the same things because they have one major thing in common: They love Jesus. Jesus calls us to love each other, and that is just what they do.

Dear God, help me to love people who are different from me in some way. May I always remember that Jesus loves us and wants us to love one another in his name. Amen.

AUGUST 21 ✳ BE A FRIEND WHO TEACHES

Let the word of Christ dwell in you richly as you teach and admonish one another with all wisdom, and as you sing psalms, hymns and spiritual songs with gratitude in your hearts to God.
—*Colossians 3:16*

When I was growing up, I loved church camp. It was a special time when I grew closer to God and developed good friendships. Singing at camp was so much fun. It was our song leader, Kelley, who made it fun. She could play anything on the piano. I wanted to be like her.

One day I asked Kelley to help me learn to play better. We talked about my piano habits and how I didn't practice for my lessons. Gently she admonished me and told me that if I ever wanted to improve, I must practice, practice, practice. Then she taught me the most useful thing. She told me that if I really wanted to be able to play anything, I should open a hymnal, learn hymn number 1, and then move on to the next hymn and the next until, finally, I could play the entire hymnal. That one "lesson" did more for my piano playing than any other!

Sometimes friends have a way of teaching us things that no one else can. What are you teaching your friends?

Dear God, thank you for friends who get me going in the right direction and teach me new things. Help me to be that kind of friend to others. Amen.

AUGUST 22 ✳ TREAT OTHERS WITH EQUAL CONCERN

But God has combined the members of the body and has given greater honor to

the parts that lacked it, so that there should be no division in the body, but that its parts should have equal concern for each other.

—*1 Corinthians 12:24b-25*

One of the best parts of camp was being part of a small group and doing group-building activities together. You might not have had many friends, or you might have been the most popular person in school, but in group-building activities, everybody was equal. There were no divisions, and everybody had to be concerned about everybody else. The "trust fall" was one of those activities. You were dependent on your group to catch you as you fell. You worked hard to catch and support others so that, in turn, you could trust them to catch you!

Our Christian faith is like that. We are all equal in the eyes of God, and we need to treat one another with equal concern; in the process, we will be building our relationship with God.

Dear God, please help me to have equal concern for all your children. Amen.

EAT WITH THOSE YOU CARE ABOUT

So then, my brothers and sisters, when you come together to eat, wait for one another. —*1 Corinthians 11:33 (NRSV)*

Wait on somebody else to eat? What a concept! We all rush around so much that we don't have time to wait, right? You may have football practice; your brother may have a piano lesson; your sister may have a Girl Scout meeting. Sitting down to eat together may be foreign to many of us, but it can be very important to us as we create a caring community.

At church camp, we all waited for the dinner bell to ring and then entered the cafeteria together, where our meals were served family style—with everything on the tables in serving dishes so that we could help ourselves. Meals were great because of the time we had together, eating and talking and laughing. In the process of eating together, we also were building relationships with one another.

Today, try "waiting for others" at mealtime—at home, at school, or wherever you may be. Slow down, talk together, laugh a little, and enjoy building relationships as you share a meal together.

Dear God, help me learn to enjoy mealtime as fellowship time with those I care about. Amen.

AUGUST 24 ✷ BE PATIENT WITH OTHERS AS YOU HELP THEM

And we urge you, brothers [and sisters], warn those who are idle, encourage the timid, help the weak, be patient with everyone. —1 Thessalonians 5:14

He was miserable. He had never been away from Mom and Dad and had no idea how to act at camp. He would not participate in anything. He was like a shy kitten, and all he wanted to do was go home. His counselor was frustrated and confused and unsure of how to deal with this camper. Then, at vespers one night, 1 Thessalonians 5:14 was read. The counselor realized that this was his answer. He must be patient with the camper and do all he could to encourage him, get him involved, and work with him diligently. So the counselor did just that, and he was successful. The camper got involved and began to make friends and by the end of the week, he did not want to go home because he was so happy at camp.

Dear God, I know you want me to help my brothers and sisters in every way I can. Please give me the patience I need, even when people frustrate me. Amen.

AUGUST 25 ✷ DON'T BE A STUMBLING BLOCK

Let us therefore no longer pass judgment on one another, but resolve instead never to put a stumbling block or hindrance in the way of another. —Romans 14:13 (NRSV)

It was the end of summer, the last week of camp. It was to be the highlight of the summer—a week of Christian growth, love, and learning. Instead, it turned into a nightmare.

That week I was supposed to feel accepted and loved—and so was everybody else—but our cabin had a group of girls who made fun of everybody (except themselves, of course). According to the "in crowd," the rest of us were weird, and they let us know it by playing all sorts of pranks on us. They put lotion in our hair while we were sleeping, covered our pillows with baby powder, and made terrible jokes about everybody. Talk about a stumbling block! I did not feel accepted and loved that week; in fact, I began to wonder if God was really at camp with us at all.

Dear God, our behavior truly can be a stumbling block to those

around us. May I never be a stumbling block to anyone; instead, show me how to help someone find the way to you. Amen.

LOVE BY LISTENING

Dear friends, let us love one another, for love comes from God. Everyone who loves has been born of God and knows God.
—1 John 4:7

My sisters and I were often impatient as teenagers. For instance, we loved being with our grandparents, and we loved the stories our grandfather told. But we really didn't listen closely. We were always thinking about our next date, or a test at school, or the TV show we might be missing.

What we missed was the love we could have been sharing. A great way to show others we love them is to listen to them—especially to those around us who are elderly. Yes, sometimes we may hear the same story over and over, but what's important is the love we share and the relationship we are building.

Dear God, today help me to love someone by listening—100 percent, true listening. Amen.

SERVE ONE ANOTHER

You . . . were called to be free. But do not use your freedom to indulge the sinful nature; rather, serve one another in love.
—Galatians 5:13

I know of a youth group that did many things together. They studied; they played; they took trips. They were a close group. Every fall they raked leaves; it was both a fundraiser and a service project. They charged most people a small fee—but not the elderly, shut-in members of the church. For them, the group would rake for free to help them out. A lot of the shut-ins would come out and talk to the youth while they raked.

This youth group provided two very important ministries. One was the ministry of assistance, which the group provided by raking the leaves. But just as important was the ministry of caring, which the group provided by listening and talking to the people they helped.

There are so many ways we can serve one another in love!

Dear God, help me and a group of my friends—whether at church or school—look for ways we can serve other people in love. Amen.

PRAY FOR OTHERS

Pray for each other so that you may be healed. — *James 5:16a*

They thought it was weird. "You do *what* for lunch on Tuesdays?" they asked.

"I go to Prayer Paracletes, a prayer group," I said.

They were confused and thought I had "lost it." So I tried to explain.

"A group from my church eats lunch together every Tuesday; and while we eat, we pray for each other, other people, the church, and the world. We do this because prayer is powerful; and if we do it together, awesome things can happen. Our prayers are not always answered in the way we want, but God does answer them.

"Some people we have prayed for have been healed. Others have found relief. We never know how God will answer our prayers, but we keep on praying.

"Prayer makes a difference. Prayer can make a difference for you, too. You want to have lunch with me on Tuesday?"

Dear God, help us to remember that we are supposed to pray for each other. And especially help us to realize how important it is for us to talk to you and share with you daily. Amen.

PRACTICE LOVING OTHERS

May the Lord make your love increase and overflow for each other and for everyone else, just as ours does for you.
—*1 Thessalonians 3:12*

Marching band in August—boy, was it hot! They were the dog days of summer, and we spent hours in the heat practicing. We sweated, we griped, we drank water, we complained—but we *practiced!* We weren't the only ones. The football team was spending hours running drills and sweating. The cheerleaders were practicing too. By the time the first ballgame came around, we were all ready—ready to cheer, ready to play, ready to march. Just imagine how things would have gone if everybody had not practiced. It would have been a mess. To do well, we had to practice.

Our relationships with God and others are like that, too. We must work on them. They don't just happen. We have to work on loving our neighbors. We have to work on treating others with love and kindness. We have to put our faith into practice.

Dear God, help me to practice loving other people every day. Make my love for others increase and overflow. Amen.

GIVE LOVE YOUR ALL

Love the LORD your God with all your heart and with all your soul and with all your strength. These commandments that I give you today are to be upon your hearts. Impress them on your children. Talk about them when you sit at home and when you walk along the road, when you lie down and when you get up. —Deuteronomy 6:5-7

"Mom, you've told me. I heard you. Leave me alone." These were the kind of words that could be heard every day in our house. In love, Mom would remind us over and over to "do this or do that," or, more often, "don't do this and don't do that." Although I knew she had my best interests in mind, it was annoying. After all, I already knew how to act!

But Mom's words of wisdom echoed in all that I said and did. Because I heard them over and over, they became part of me. The scriptures repeat certain words of wisdom again and again throughout the Bible. For instance, what Jesus called the greatest commandment was given to the people of God long before Jesus was born; yet Jesus lived it out in his life— perhaps because it was repeated over and over until it became part of his life. And Jesus wants this commandment to become part of us, to become who we are as his disciples.

> **Dear God, help me to be a true follower of Christ. May your commandment to love one another always be a part of who I am as a disciple of Jesus Christ. Amen.**

RECOGNIZE THE GREATEST GIFT

For God so loved the world that he gave his one and only Son, that whoever believes in him shall not perish but have eternal life. —John 3:16

What is the greatest gift you have ever received? Think about it—the *best* gift, the one you wanted the most, the one you treasured the most. At one time, mine was the letter jacket with the school's name and my name on the back. I wanted that jacket so much that I thought the world would end if I didn't get it! I earned my jacket, and I thought I was cool. I fit in with the crowd.

Gradually, through the years, I have discovered that the jacket is not the best gift I have ever received—or ever will receive. The best gift is the gift of Jesus Christ. Jesus gave his life for me. Even though I did not deserve it, Jesus gave it for me. The least I can do for Jesus is to love others. That is my gift back to Jesus. I love others because he first loved me.

> **Dear God, thank you for my greatest gift. Help me to love others the way you have loved me. Amen.**

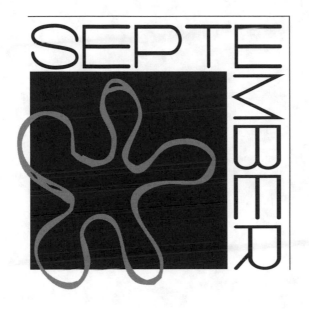

SEPTEMBER

NATHANIEL'S STORY

Reginia Guess

NATHANIEL'S STORY

Reginia Guess

SEEING BEYOND LIMITS

"For I know the plans I have for you," declares the LORD*, "plans to prosper you and not to harm you, plans to give you hope and a future."*
—*Jeremiah 29:11*

My name is Nate. That's short for Nathaniel. I live in the heart of the city. It's a place that people glance at from their car windows as they speed along the Interstate. A place where the grass and concrete compete for space, just like the people who live here. I'm sixteen years old, and I have a younger brother and a younger sister. We live with our mother. My father has his own problems, so he is in and out of my life—mostly out. My mother never finished high school, but she is one of the smartest people I know. I should listen to her more. She tells me that I will make it out of here. I want to believe her.

> **Heavenly Father, help me to see and believe in your vision when all I can see is limits. Amen.**

LOOKING FOR AN ANSWER

Call to me and I will answer you and tell you great and unsearchable things you do not know.
—*Jeremiah 33:3*

I'm staring at the sky, wishing. The movement of clouds is awesome. They look so free. I close my eyes and imagine myself flying high, carried farther and farther away by a crisp, cool wind. When I mess up, that is exactly what I want to do: fly away. It never works for me. I just seem to dig myself in deeper and deeper. I don't know what I can do to make things better. I tell myself that if I talk to someone about it, they may think I'm stupid or weak. I'm so used to handling my own problems. I need an answer. I know that running away is not it.

Dear God, when I am uncertain about what I should do, let my first step be a prayer to you. Amen.

NEEDING GOD'S COMFORT

My soul is weary with sorrow; strengthen me according to your word. —Psalm 119:28

I'm Arlene, Nathaniel's mother. My children are my life. Through them I hope to realize all the dreams that never happened for me. Living here is not easy. I want a better life for my children. Nathaniel has the potential to do great things. He has a curious mind, always thinking. Lately I've been feeling like I am losing him. I see him changing, growing bitter. I'm sure that it's about his father. He won't talk to me about it. Maybe he blames me. Some of the things he has done have truly disappointed me. It's hard for me to trust him. My fear is that no matter what I do, the streets will claim my children.

Lord, thank you for comforting me in times of trouble, and for strengthening me through your word. Amen.

CARRYING HEAVY BURDENS

Look to the LORD and his strength; seek his face always. Remember the wonders he has done. —Psalm 105:4-5a

It's Arlene again, Nathaniel's mother. I still remember hearing the sound of the telephone ringing. A cold chill went through me. Something inside of me knew that it was about Nathaniel. I thought the worst. When the person speaking told me that Nathaniel had been arrested, my heart stopped beating. My mouth went dry, and I could barely speak. I listened, and I thought about all the things I've said—sometimes even preached—to Nathaniel about the fast life. I've taught my children right from wrong, raised them in a Christian home. Still, none of that prevented the phone call I'd always dreaded. I was living my nightmare. The only thing I knew to do was to call on the name of Jesus.

172

Almighty God, when my burden is too heavy to bear, I'm thankful that I can come to you and leave it there. Amen.

STANDING IN TIMES OF TRIAL

Consider it pure joy . . . whenever you face trials of many kinds, because you know that the testing of your faith develops persever-ance.　　　　　　　　　　　　　　　　　　*—James 1:2-3*

I was nervous about coming back to school. No one at school has really said anything to me about what happened over the summer. I talk about it with some of my friends, if they ask. I try not to bring it up. It's not something I want to brag about. It's really something I want to forget. I've noticed some strange looks. Walking down the hallway today I overheard some students making jokes about it. I didn't snap, but I felt like leaving school and never coming back.

God, with you beside me, though I stumble, I will not fall. Help me to stand in times of trial. Amen.

MAKING CHOICES

Choose my instruction instead of silver, knowledge rather than choice gold.　　　　　　　　　　　　　　　　*—Proverbs 8:10*

It was loud and noisy on the bus, and the ride seemed like forever. Since I didn't feel like talking to anyone, I sat in the seat that's usually empty: the one behind Mr. Johnson, our bus driver. He likes to talk a lot. I told him that I didn't want to talk, that I had a lot on my mind. I stared out the window. That didn't stop Mr. Johnson. The next thing I knew, he started telling me a story about an accident he almost had with a large tree trunk in the road.

"At that moment I had to decide whether to go over it or around it," he said. "If I went over it, I knew it would cause more damage, so I went around it. Never let things stand in your way. You always have a choice."

Heavenly Father, when my way is dark and I don't know what choice to make, I know you will provide the light to guide me along my path. Amen.

HAVING FAITH

Now faith is being sure of what we hope for and certain of what we do not see.
                                                    —Hebrews 11:1

From the bus, I can hear my neighborhood long before I'm able to see it in the early morning darkness. Roaring car engines and honking horns quickly change to the sound of rap and salsa music. The daytime sounds are different from the sounds at night. At night, it's hard for me to study and finish my homework. I hear police sirens, gunshots, and loud conversations. There are nights when I can hardly sleep. A bullet doesn't have anyone's name on it. Sometimes I'll sleep on the floor to be safe. People who don't live here think you just get used to it. How do you get used to war? I don't think I'll ever get used to it. I don't want to.

I trust you, Lord, and believe that my circumstances will change. Help me to hold on. Amen.

HOLDING ON TO HOPE

For nothing is impossible with God.   —Luke 1:37

My mind just seems to drift. I think about living someplace else. Living here has a lot to do with the problems I have. From my porch, I watch as people drive away from the city. I want to go with them. One day I'll drive past here on my way to a quieter place. I want to go to college so that I can own my own business.

My mother struggles to make it. I thought that by bringing in some extra money, things would be better. I saw a lot of people around here making money that way. I figured I could do it for a short time. I got caught. If we moved, things would be better.

God, keep reminding me that all things are possible with you because you are the way, the truth, and the light. Amen.

DREAMING OF A BETTER LIFE

"Again, I tell you that if two of you on earth agree about anything you ask for, it will be done for you by my Father in heaven."
                                                    —Matthew 18:19

Success and respect is what I want. Once I make it out of here, I'm coming back to my neighborhood and cleaning it up. I'll build a new community center for all the kids, a theater, and a supermarket. That way the people who live here won't have to ride the bus to another area to buy food. No guns or drugs will be allowed. Security will check on this regularly. Everyone will have a job, and the grace period for runaway fathers will be over. I'm just dreaming.

Heavenly Father, grant me the power to change my life and move in a positive direction. I have faith that you will answer me, because your Word promises you will grant requests made in line with your will. Amen.

SEPTEMBER 10 WANTING TO CHANGE

So do not fear, for I am with you; do not be dismayed, for I am your God. I will strengthen you and help you; I will uphold you with my righteous right hand. —Isaiah 41:10

I'm Robert, Nathan's father. I got off track. I'll admit that. At the time, I thought that leaving would be best for my family. I chose to be selfish, and now I see that it caused my family great pain. I don't know if things will ever be the same again. In time I hope to make things right. They've heard it all before. There is a difference this time; I've reached out for help. It's going to be a long road back home. I've got to make it. This time I know I'm not alone on my journey. I went over to Arlene's today to see the children. Nate wasn't there.

Lord, your mercy is infinite. Direct my path and order my steps in your Word. Amen.

SEPTEMBER 11 HONORING MY PARENTS

"Honor your father and your mother, as the LORD your God has commanded you, so that you may live long and that it may go well with you in the land the LORD your God is giving you." —Deuteronomy 5:16

I can always tell when Pops has been here. I could feel it when I walked in the door. No matter how much she tries to hide it, I always know. Mom was looking sad, and I could tell that she had been crying. I didn't say any-thing—just headed straight for my room and slammed the door shut. An envelope was on my bed. It didn't take much to figure out who it was from. I shook my head. He shows up whenever he feels like it and expects every-one to be excited to see him. I'm glad I wasn't at home.

Dear God, help me to honor my parents—even when I don't like what they say or do; even when I don't think they deserve my respect. Amen.

LISTENING AND UNDERSTANDING

My child, if you accept my words and treasure up my command-ments within you, making your ear attentive to wisdom and inclining your heart to understanding; . . . then you will understand the fear of the LORD *and find the knowledge of God.* —Proverbs 2:1-2, 5 (NRSV)

It feels like that letter has zapped all the air out of my room. I'm not sure what to do with it. I could throw it away. It's not like I don't know what's in there. I should throw it away. It's probably more "sorry this" and "sorry that." Same old thing. I'm going to throw it away. The envelope looks wrin-kled. It looks like he's been carrying it around for a while in his pocket. He probably had someone else write it. I ought to throw it away. I don't have to read it. But it could be good for a few laughs. When I'm ready, I'll read it and then throw it away.

Lord, please bless me with ears to listen and an open heart to understand. Amen.

SURRENDERING TO GOD

The human mind plans the way, but the LORD *directs the steps.* —Proverbs 16:9 (NRSV)

Nate,
Please read this. There's a lot I want to say to you. The past few years have been rough on the family, I know. Most of it has to do with me and the prob-lems I've had. If I could change all of that, I would. What I can do is just get my life in order. I'm doing that now, Nate. I've turned to God and found a

church home (yeah, even me), and I'm looking really hard for a steady job. I've been going to these meetings, and it's helped me to stop drinking. I know you got into some trouble. I'm proud of how you've come through it. I'm sorry for the pain I've caused you. I hope in time you will forgive me.

Pops

Heavenly Father, today I surrender all to you, and through you I gain all. Amen.

SEEKING GOD'S WILL

He went away a second time and prayed, "My Father, if it is not possible for this cup to be taken away unless I drink it, may your will be done." —Matthew 26:42

It's Arlene, Nathaniel's mother. Nathaniel has not mentioned the letter to me. I don't think he's read it. I'm tired of being in the middle, trying to keep the peace between them. This time I'm staying out of it.

Nathaniel's father needs him as much as Nathaniel needs his father. It's painful to watch someone you love self-destruct. It brings up a lot of emotions. Sooner or later you have to make a choice. I chose my family. I never thought I would have to break up my family to keep my family.

Heavenly Father, help me to remember "your will be done"—not my own—and help me to know what your will is. Amen.

HAVING TROUBLE BELIEVING

For God so loved the world that he gave his one and only Son, that whoever believes in him shall not perish but have eternal life. For God did not send his Son into the world to condemn the world, but to save the world through him. —John 3:16-17

I used to believe. I went to church. I sang the songs. I said all the right words. Then I started looking around here. I saw the crime, the drugs, the fighting, and the people with no jobs. I decided that maybe God's forgotten us. I stopped praying. I still go to church; I have to—Mom's house rules. But it's like I'm there and not there. I want to believe again. I *need* to believe again, 'cause I know I've done some wrong things. I never meant to break my mom's trust in me.

God, help me to remember that you never break your promises

to me—even when it's hard for me to keep believing—and that you sacrificed your Son to forgive all my sins. Amen.

SEPTEMBER 16 — LETTING GO OF VENGEFUL FEELINGS

Love is patient, love is kind. It does not envy, it does not boast, it is not proud. It is not rude, it is not self-seeking, it is not easily angered, it keeps no record of wrongs.
—*1 Corinthians 13:4-5*

All I've thought about today is that letter. I've gotten angrier and angrier just thinking about it. I really should just throw it away—just like he did me, like he did all of us. I don't need him. The longer I wait to read it, the more he'll wonder. I kind of like that idea. He doesn't have a clue about what it's been like for us, especially for Mom. Yep, I'm just going to take my time, make him feel what we've been feeling.

Lord, help me to see that vengeful thoughts keep me in bondage and separate me from the true spirit of your love. Amen.

SEPTEMBER 17 — UNWILLING TO FORGIVE

Be kind and compassionate to one another, forgiving each other, just as in Christ God forgave you. —*Ephesians 4:32*

The curiosity got to me. I opened the letter. I'm not sure what I am supposed to feel, because he's asking me to understand things I can't. All I know is that he hasn't been around like he should. My mother tries her best, but there are some things I can only learn from a man. I'm having to figure them out on my own. He wants forgiveness and another chance. I'm not sure if I can give it. His problems have hurt our family. All this anger wells up inside me when I think about it. It makes me want to explode.

Dear God, being human means we make mistakes; teach me to forgive others as you have forgiven me. Amen.

HAVING COMPASSION

"Renounce your sins by doing what is right, and your wickedness by being kind to the oppressed." —Daniel 4:27

The streets will swallow you up. I can see it in the eyes and on the faces of the men who hang out on the street corners. They look like life has beaten them down and their dreams have been chewed up in bits and pieces until nothing is left. "Stay in those books, Jr." they say as I walk past them on the way to the bus stop. It makes me nervous seeing them just standing there. Is there a space reserved for me? That's definitely not what I want. I think about their faces on the bus ride to school.

Heavenly Father, let my efforts at progress never overshadow my compassion for others whose choices and options may be different from mine. Amen.

SEEKING RECONCILIATION

So when you are offering your gift at the altar, if you remember that your brother or sister has something against you, leave your gift there before the altar and go; first be reconciled to your brother or sister, and then come and offer your gift. —Matthew 5:23-24 (NRSV)

It's Robert, Nate's father. An important part of my recovery is trying to reconcile with the people I have harmed. I started with Arlene, Nate's mother, then Nate, and finally the younger children. I wrote Nate a letter because I knew that he would not listen to me in person. With Arlene, I had to do it face to face. She has had so much on her shoulders, having to do it all herself. I didn't really know what to say. It was hard for me to look at her. The first thing I said was, "Arlene, I'm sorry." I didn't get much else out. She cried. I cried. It blew me away when she told me that she had forgiven me a long time ago. I still haven't heard from Nate. I don't even know if he's read the letter. I hope he will.

Help me to reconcile with those I have wronged, Lord, and grant me patience to wait on your timing for full reconciliation, because your time is always the right time. Amen.

STEPPING OUT IN FAITH

For we walk by faith, not by sight.
—2 Corinthians 5:7 (NRSV)

The older people who have lived here for a long time say this used to be a good place to live. They say there were trees and grass and space for children to play without being afraid. I try to picture it in my mind—to see how it was and not how it is. If people started caring more, it could be that way again. I'm going to start by pulling out weeds in my yard. Maybe later on I will plant some flowers. Maybe that's what happened. Everybody was waiting on somebody else to do things, so nothing got done.

God, give me the courage and conviction to step out in faith, even when no one else will follow. Amen.

PRESSING ON . . . ONE DAY AT A TIME

Forgetting what is behind and straining toward what is ahead, I press on toward the goal to win the prize for which God has called me heavenward in Christ Jesus. —Philippians 3:13b-14

There are several crumpled up letters in my waste paper basket. Some are long and some are short. I knew that writing him back wouldn't be easy. I had to stop a few times when I was writing because my eyes started watering . . . from eyelashes getting caught in my eye. The more I wrote, the better I felt. I was able to let go of some of the anger I've been feeling for a long time. I'm going to send this last one. I'm tired of feeling this way.

Dear God, help me to let go of the past and live one day at a time, pressing on toward the future you are calling me to. Amen.

LEARNING TO FORGIVE

For if you forgive [others] when they sin against you, your heavenly Father will also forgive you. —Matthew 6:14

Pops,

Your letter looked old. I guess you'd been carrying it around a while. Sounds like church and those meeting you go to are working for you. That's good. You've hurt me; I won't lie. But I'm not that angry about it anymore. It forced me to step up to the plate and be the man of the house. I know that Mom told you about the trouble I got into last summer. All I can say is that I learned. I don't want to spend my life locked up. I don't want people to judge me by the mistake I made. I don't know if that is forgiveness. It's all I have right now.

Nate

Heavenly Father, help me to forgive others—for as I forgive, I am forgiven. Amen.

SEEKING GOD'S GUIDANCE

Jesus answered, "It is written: '[One] does not live on bread alone, but on every word that comes from the mouth of God.' "
—*Matthew 4:4*

I came so close to not mailing the letter to Pops. When I finally decided that I would, I couldn't find a stamp. Then the rain started pouring down outside. I really didn't want to go to the mailbox for one letter. All of a sudden I remembered Mr. Johnson's tree trunk story, and before I knew it, I was at the mailbox. I felt light as a feather after I put that letter into the mailbox slot. It felt good.

God, I don't wish for a way to escape from my problems anymore, but I do pray for your guidance. Speak to me through your Word today. Amen.

BELIEVING I CAN DO IT

If God is for us, who can be against us?   —*Romans 8:31b*

If I learned anything this summer, it's that I don't want to be locked up for the rest of my life. I don't want to have to ask permission from another person to do simple things, personal things. When I was locked up, I read books to make the time go faster. Most of the books I read were about people who had a lot of things stacked against them but came out okay. I can relate. Some of them even lived in neighborhoods like this one. Their stories helped me to believe that if they can do it, so can I. I need something to believe in.

God, help me recognize the barriers I put before myself and choose to live a different way, believing that it's truly possible because you are on my side. Amen.

 # FACING MY FEARS AND TAKING ACTION

Cast your bread upon the waters, for after many days you will find it again.　　　　　　　　　　　　　　*—Ecclesiastes 11:1*

I'm going to tell my mom today that I've read the letter and that I've written back. I've avoided it, but I know I've got to do this. I want her to hear it from me first. I just don't want her to get her hopes up, thinking that this is going to make us father and son again. It's just what it is: two people trying to talk. I don't want any pressure to give something I can't give. Things are starting to turn around for me. It feels good.

Dear God, help me to face my fears and take whatever action you are calling me to take. Amen.

 # ACKNOWLEDGING GOD'S SOVEREIGNTY

For there is nothing hidden that will not be disclosed, and nothing concealed that will not be known or brought out into the open.
—Luke 8:17

It's Arlene, Nathaniel's mother. Nathaniel told me about the letter he wrote his father. I was washing dishes and nearly dropped one on the floor when he told me that not only had he read the letter but also he had written one back. I tried hard not to make a big deal of it; but before I knew it, I heard myself say out loud, "Praise God!" Nathaniel laughed and laughed. It was music to my ears. It's been a long time since I've heard him laugh like that. I'm so glad he told me. It took great courage to do what he did. I am very proud of him. I told him so.

Heavenly Father, you alone are sovereign. When I am doubtful, restore my faith, for nothing is hidden from you. Amen.

CHANGING

The one who began a good work among you will bring it to completion by the day of Jesus Christ. —Philippians 1:6 (NRSV)

My situation at school is getting better. Rumors around here don't last long before they move on to someone else. There are some people who are still curious. They want to know what it's like to be locked up. I'm just trying to get my grades up and put all that behind me. It's not anything I want to brag about. Things like that used to make me just want to go off or escape. It's different now. I can feel myself changing, even if other people don't see it.

Thank you, God, for accepting me just as I am, and for having patience with me as I become all you want me to be. Amen.

PRAYING FOR ONE ANOTHER

Therefore confess your sins to one another, and pray for one another, so that you may be healed. The prayer of the righteous is powerful and effective. —James 5:16 (NRSV)

It's Arlene, Nathaniel's mother. I can see the change in Nathaniel—more and more every day. It's like his spirit has been set free. His anger kept him in bondage for so long. I've prayed about this, and the Lord has answered my prayers. Maybe it can never be like it was, but I think he is open to a relationship with his father. The changes in him are having a positive effect on his younger brother and sister. I hear them talking in the yard as they help him. He's calmer with them. I feel like I can trust him again.

Heavenly Father, thank you for reminding me of the power of prayer. When I hold on to your unchanging hand, anything is possible. Amen.

SEPTEMBER 29
TRUSTING GOD TO BRING GOOD FROM ANY CIRCUMSTANCE

And we know that in all things God works for the good of those who love him.
—*Romans 8:28*

It's Robert, Nate's father. I wasn't sure that Nate would write me back. And I thought that if he did, he would really let me have it. I read the letter over and over. A lot has happened. Some things I can make better, and some I can't. But I have been blessed with an opportunity, and I am grateful. It's a beginning, a place to start. I found my faith during the lowest point in my life. Nate will find his own way in his own time.

Almighty God, all I need to do is keep on looking to you, because you can bring good from any situation or circumstance. Amen.

SEPTEMBER 30
TRUSTING GOD FOR THE FUTURE

Trust in the LORD with all your heart and lean not on your own understanding; in all your ways acknowledge him, and he will make your paths straight.
—*Proverbs 3:5-6*

While working in my yard, I've noticed something strange: Grass grows in between the cracks in the concrete. Sometimes even a flower gets through.

This may not be the best place to live, but I can still grow here. And I don't have to live here forever. There's something I feel is certain: If I give up and try to escape by living the fast life, I *will* stay here. My dreams are too big for street corners.

Dear God, help me to find my way in this world, knowing that your hand will always be there to guide me and lift me up when I fall. Amen.

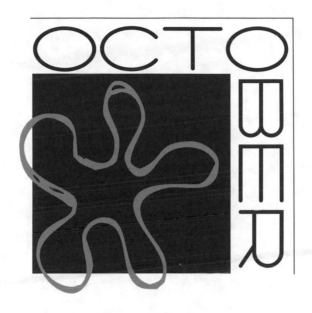

WHAT DOES IT
MEAN TO BE A
DISCIPLE OF
CHRIST?

John William Peterson

WHAT DOES IT MEAN TO BE A DISCIPLE OF CHRIST?

John William Peterson

ACCEPTING GOD'S GRACE

Then he poured water into a basin and began to wash the disciples' feet and to wipe them with the towel that was tied around him. . . . Peter said to him, "You will never wash my feet." Jesus answered, "Unless I wash you, you have no share with me." Simon Peter said to him, "Lord, not my feet only but also my hands and my head!"

— John 13:5, 8-9 (NRSV)

On the last night of camp, I found myself in a circle of people—my "family" for the week. We were bringing camp to a close with a foot washing service. As the person beside me slid my feet into a basin of water, I remember thinking that, like Peter, I didn't deserve to have Christ wash my feet. After all, I was a nerdy, fat kid who'd never measured high on my school's popularity meter. How could Jesus care about me?

Suddenly, as the cloth caressed my foot, I realized that none of us were worthy—that this was the point. Jesus loved me not because I deserved it, but simply because I was a child of God. Overwhelmed by the realization that I didn't have to measure up any longer, I was filled with joy. In actions deeper than words, Jesus demonstrated the gift of amazing love and grace offered to each one of us. Accepting this gift is the first step in becoming a disciple of Jesus Christ.

This month we will explore what it means to be a disciple of Christ. By doing so, we are beginning a journey together—a journey towards hope, love, and unending joy.

Dear Jesus, thank you for loving me. Help me accept your gift of grace and share it with others by following your example. Amen.

HAVING POSITIVE SELF-WORTH

For God so loved the world that he gave his only Son, so that everyone who believes in him may not perish but may have eternal life.
—John 3:16 (NRSV)

Ellen's mother sat down beside her on the bed. "Honey, why aren't you eating?"

"I eat plenty," Ellen replied.

"Excuse me, but that's just not true," her mother said. "Is something wrong, El?"

After a moment's hesitation, Ellen muttered, "I'm too fat."

"But you're not!" protested her mother.

"I am! I'm a fat pig! I hate the way I look!" cried Ellen.

Unfortunately, Ellen is not alone. One study conducted by the University of Arizona found that 90 percent of girls surveyed expressed dissatisfaction with their own bodies. Such preoccupation with one's physical image carries a heavy price. An article I read several years ago reported that eating disorders are estimated to affect approximately two million teenage girls and half a million boys.

Christianity carries the key to feeling good about ourselves. As children of God, we know ourselves to be loved unconditionally. We call this undeserved love "grace"—an eternal gift of self-worth which is ours through good times and bad. Praise be to God!

Dear God, thank you for loving me just the way I am. Amen.

HEARING GOD'S CALL

God called to [Moses] out of the bush. . . . "The cry of the Israelites has now come to me; I have also seen how the Egyptians oppress them. So come, I will send you to Pharaoh to bring my people, the Israelites, out of Egypt."
—Exodus 3:4, 9-10 (NRSV)

A young Indian attorney boarded a train in South Africa. Upon finding the "colored" man sitting in the first-class coach, an Afrikaaner complained to railroad officers, who asked the attorney to change compartments. He refused, politely showing his first-class ticket. At the next station, he was thrown from the train. Years later, Mahatma Gandhi recalled that experience as the most important of his life. It was a minor incident, and yet it set Gandhi on the path of social justice.

For each of us, God's call to discipleship is different. Moses received his call from a voice within a burning bush; Gandhi's came with a swift kick to his behind. However the call comes, each is valid.

What is God calling *you* to this day? To listen to a friend? To befriend a stranger? To dry a tear? Whatever the task, know that God is with you.

Dear Jesus, help me to hear your call to discipleship—today and every day. Amen.

 # LISTENING TO GOD

[Martha] had a sister named Mary, who sat at the Lord's feet and listened to what he was saying. But Martha was distracted by her many tasks; so she came to [Jesus] and asked, "Lord, do you not care that my sister has left me to do all the work by myself? Tell her then to help me." But the Lord answered her, "Martha, Martha, you are worried and distracted by many things; there is need of only one thing. Mary has chosen the better part, which will not be taken away from her."
—Luke 10:39-42 (NRSV)

Veronica Vega was a 4.0 student when she started working afternoons, evenings, and weekends. Now she pays for her phone bill, car insurance, the latest fashion trends, and her evenings out with friends. She's paying in other ways too.

Dragging home from her checking job at a local grocery at 11:00 P.M., she takes caffeine pills to stay awake, calls a few friends, and begins her homework. Usually she falls asleep on top of her books—her alarm set for 6:00 A.M. "I have major bags under my eyes," she says, "but I don't want to give up the little luxuries I have." (Miriam Bensimhon and Andy Levin, "The Exhausting Days and Sleepless Nights of a Working Teenager," *Life Magazine* 16 [July 1993]: 74 [6]).

Like Martha, Veronica has become preoccupied with the daily grind. She no longer has time to listen to the voice of God. However busy our schedules may be, we must carve out moments for daily prayer. To do otherwise is to lose touch with the very source of our being.

What's blocking your ability to listen?

Dear Lord, help me to make time for listening to you. Amen.

OCTOBER 5
LEARNING TO PRAY

[Jesus] was praying in a certain place, and after he had finished, one of his disciples said to him, "Lord, teach us to pray, as John taught his disciples." He said to them, "When you pray, say: Father, hallowed be your name. Your kingdom come. Give us each day our daily bread. And forgive us our sins, for we ourselves forgive everyone indebted to us. And do not bring us to the time of trial." —Luke 11:1-4 (NRSV)

When Jesus returned from praying, his disciples asked him to teach them how to pray. Jesus responded with the Lord's Prayer.

Let's consider two things we can learn from this passage. First, your prayer life deepens with practice. Judging from the disciples' question and Jesus' response, none of them thought of prayer as something that can be accomplished without effort. Have you ever been reluctant to say a prayer in public because you didn't know what to say? We all have! Becoming comfortable with prayer takes time, and we get better at it with practice.

Second, Jesus believed in petitionary prayer—prayer that makes requests of God. Just take a look at the Lord's Prayer: After the first sentence, which is a statement of praise and adoration, every sentence is a request—not for selfish desires, but for God's desires for us. Jesus said, "Ask, and it will be given you; search, and you will find" (Matthew 7:7 NRSV). If you want to grow in your faith, then pray about it! God will answer your requests.

Dear Jesus, as you did so long ago for your first disciples, teach me to pray so that my life will glorify you. Amen.

OCTOBER 6
STRIVING FIRST FOR THE KINGDOM OF GOD

Therefore do not worry, saying, "What will we eat?" or "What will we drink?" or "What will we wear?" For it is the Gentiles who strive for all these things; and indeed your heavenly Father knows that you need all these things. But strive first for the kingdom of God and his righteousness, and all these things will be given to you as well. —Matthew 6:31-33 (NRSV)

In Detroit, a teen was shot for his basketball shoes. In Fort Lauderdale, a fifteen-year-old student was robbed for his gold chain. In Oxon Hill, Maryland, a seventeen-year-old honor student was killed during the robbery of another student's designer jacket. Behind tragic headlines such as these lies the craving to fit in. Unable to afford popularity's price tag, some are even driven to crime.

We are all guilty of judging others by their outward appearances. School can be a cruel place where persons are put down not because of who they are but because of what they wear.

It was no different in Jesus' day. Persons, consumed with anxiety about daily existence, forgot the one thing that offers true joy: the kingdom of God. Spend your energy pursuing your relationship with God, said Jesus, and the rest will fall into place. It's a message we'd all do well to remember.

Dear Jesus, keep my mind and heart focused not on outward appearances but on your kingdom. Amen.

OCTOBER 7
LIVING A LIFE OF HUMILITY

He has told you, O mortal, what is good; and what does the LORD *require of you but to . . . walk humbly with your God?*
—Micah 6:8 (NRSV)

"Lifeboats?" said Mrs. Astor. "Isn't the Titanic unsinkable?" She and her husband, John Astor, stood on the deck of the oceanliner with First Officer Murdock.

"She is unsinkable, Madam," said Murdock.

"He is correct, Mrs. Astor," said a deep voice. The party turned and found Captain Smith standing behind them. "God himself could not sink this ship," he said.

Thanks to Leonardo and cast, you know the rest of the story. Two hours after striking an iceberg, the Titanic slipped beneath the waves. Ever since, the word Titanic has been synonymous with human pride.

Perhaps Captain Smith should have read Genesis. Adam and Eve's snack was all about securing the knowledge of God for themselves—in order to be like God (see Genesis 3:2-6).

As Christ's disciples, we are required to walk humbly with our God. When we forget this biblical truth, it's time to head for the lifeboats.

Dear Lord, curb my pride today so that I may walk humbly with you. Amen.

OCTOBER 8
WELCOMING THE OUTCAST

The Pharisees and their scribes were complaining to his disciples, saying, "Why do you eat and drink with tax collectors and sinners?" Jesus answered, "Those who are well have no need of a physician, but

those who are sick; I have come to call not the righteous but sinners to repen-
tance."
                                                    —*Luke 5:30-32 (NRSV)*

"Crazy Eddie" is holding court. Each weekend a different audience of teens gathers to hear his words. Pastor Urness has brought another group of nervous church kids to meet his old friend.

Eddie, wearing a soiled jacket to ward off the evening chill, tells the youth to stay in school, in short, not to end up like him—homeless. "God doesn't want anyone to live like this," he says.

After his listeners have moved on, Eddie, as he does every night, spreads out his bag on the concrete and tries to sleep. Perhaps, if he's lucky, he'll dream of a time when hope existed. Eddie has severe claustrophobia and refuses to set foot in the homeless shelter at which Pastor Urness is chaplain. As difficult as it is for us to understand, he prefers to sleep on the streets.

Jesus reached out to the Eddies of this world—tax collectors, prostitutes, and lepers. These outcasts moved on the fringe of society, shunned by "the good people." Yet Jesus cared.

Who are the outcasts who live on the fringe of your world? And how can you reach out to them?

Dear Lord, help me to share your love with the "outcasts" of my world. Amen.

CARING FOR CHILDREN

Jesus said, "Let the little children come to me, and do not stop them; for it is to such as these that the kingdom of heaven belongs."
                                                    —*Matthew 19:14 (NRSV)*

Jesus said children have a special place in God's heart. In fact, he said that to them the kingdom of God belongs. Being a follower of Jesus means caring about what Jesus cared about. So we should be particularly concerned about the welfare of children.

What are you doing to aid neglected children? Can you spare a couple of hours a week to tutor a young student? to befriend a lonely child? to help a homeless child? to sponsor a poor boy or girl overseas? Remember, God doesn't ask us to be super heroes—just faithful. We can't save all the children of the world, but we *can* make a difference—one child at a time.

Dear Jesus, help me to welcome and love the children of the world as you did. Amen.

OCTOBER 10 STANDING UP TO PEER PRESSURE

Do not be conformed to this world, but be transformed by the renewing of your minds, so that you may discern what is the will of God—what is good and acceptable and perfect. —Romans 12:2 (NRSV)

Todd's descent into drug abuse began with a little help from his friends. "When I took the Quaaludes, everyone else was taking them, so I did too. It was the same thing with cigarettes. I just started because everyone else was smoking them. It wasn't just one or two people. It was everyone I know. I'd go to a party and the whole place would be an ashtray" (David Elkind, *All Grown Up and No Place to Go: Teenagers in Crisis*, [Redding, Mass: Addison-Wesley Publishing, 1984], 170).

Sometimes the pressure to compromise our ideals can be overwhelming. This is true at any age, but especially in the teen years. Following Jesus means having the strength of our convictions. How you choose to live your life is a witness to others. Choose well.

Dear Jesus, help me stand up to peer pressure today, so that I may witness to your abiding love. Amen.

OCTOBER 11 BEING A PEACEMAKER

Blessed are the peacemakers, for they will be called children of God. —Matthew 5:9 (NRSV)

We live in an increasingly violent society. Jack Marple, former deputy commissioner of the NYPD and author of *Crimefighter*, reports that violent crime in the United States is 3.5 times higher today than it was in 1961. This grim statistic might lead some to despair. But as disciples of Jesus Christ, we don't have that luxury. Whether or not peace will become a reality depends on us.

Each small act of kindness makes a difference. According to Marian Wright Edelman, "Helping does not require wealth or great power. It takes caring, hard work, and persistence" (Amy Hatkoff and Karen Kelly Klopp, *How to Save the Children,* [New York: Simon and Schuster, Inc., 1992]). Each of us can contribute to God's vision of peace—in our homes, our schools, and our communities—by dedicating our time, our energy, and our gifts. How will you be a peacemaker today?

Dear Jesus, lead me in the path of peace. Amen.

LOVING OTHERS

Beloved, since God loved us so much, we also ought to love one another. No one has ever seen God; if we love one another, God lives in us, and his love is perfected in us.
—*1 John 4:11-12 (NRSV)*

Moved by the plight of the Bosnian refugees, young Amity Weiss founded her own Bosnia committee, which organized fundraisers for Bosnian children. When she reached the seventh grade, Amity then founded KIDSREACH, which has raised over $45,000 for the refugees.

Amity, now fourteen, plans to continue to work with KIDSREACH until she goes to college. But helping people will always be a part of her life. "Bad things happen when good people do nothing," says Amity. "If I didn't volunteer, I'd feel as if I were taking from the world and not giving anything back" ("Daring to Care," *Seventeen* [June 1998)]: 170).

What does it mean to be a disciple of Christ? It means helping others. How is Christ's love being perfected in you?

Dear Jesus, give me opportunities to serve and love others. Amen.

ENDURING SUFFERING

In the wilderness . . . you saw how the Lord your God carried you, just as one carries a child, all the way that you traveled until you reached this place.   —*Deuteronomy 1:31 (NRSV)*

Rabbi Harold Kushner lost his young son to an incurable disease. Instead of despairing, he praised God's steadfast presence with him during his ordeal. In his book *Why Do Bad Things Happen to Good People?* (New York: Avon Books, 1981), he writes: "When people who were never strong become strong in adversity, I have to ask myself where they got these qualities. My answer is that this is how God helps us when we suffer beyond the limits of our own strength."

Each of us has wilderness experiences—times of loss and pain. Clearly, as we learn from the lives of the disciples, being a Christian carries no guarantee against suffering. In fact, though it is a source of deep joy, discipleship also entails suffering for others just as Jesus did.

The good news of the gospel is that, like Israel, when we are in the wilderness, we're never alone. For it is at the very moment when our strength fails that God carries us like a child.

Dear God, I trust you to carry me through the wilderness periods of my life. Amen.

OCTOBER 14 — OVERCOMING OBSTACLES

Recall those earlier days when, after you had been enlightened, you endured a hard struggle. . . . Do not, therefore, abandon that confidence of yours; it brings a great reward. For you need endurance, so that when you have done the will of God, you may receive what was promised.
—Hebrews 10:32, 35-36 (NRSV)

While she was growing up, downhill racer Muffy Davis dreamed of competing in the Olympics. Then, on February 4, 1989, she hit a tree at sixty miles an hour. The impact shattered both her spine and her dream. Sixteen-year-old Muffy would never walk again.

It appeared her skiing career was finished. But Muffy, returning to the slopes on a "monochair," eventually won a place on the Olympic Disabled Ski Team. Against all odds, she fulfilled her dream of competing for gold in the Nagano Olympics.

We've all been confronted by obstacles. Perhaps our test wasn't as severe as Muffy's crippling injury, but nonetheless we each have felt a measure of her frustration and pain. As Christ's disciples, we have been given the strength to overcome obstacles. Jesus himself overcame defeat on the cross "for the sake of the joy that was set before him" (Hebrews 12:2 NRSV). In his victory, we find our own.

Dear Jesus, help me to overcome the obstacles I face—today and every day. Amen.

OCTOBER 15 — TRANSFORMING FAILURE INTO SUCCESS

Two of them were going to a village called Emmaus. . . . Jesus himself came near and went with them, but their eyes were kept from recognizing him. And he said to them, "What are you discussing with each other while you walk along?" They stood still, looking sad. Then one of them . . . answered him, "Are you the only stranger in Jerusalem who does not know the things . . . about Jesus of Nazareth, who was a prophet mighty in deed and word before God and all the people, and how our chief priests and leaders handed him over to be condemned to death and

crucified him. But we had hoped that he was the one to redeem Israel."
—Luke 24:13, 15-21 (NRSV)

Joseph stood in disbelief. As the team's field goal kicker, he hadn't let them down all year. Yet today, on the last play of the last game, he hooked what could have been the game winner. His team, which had won all their games, would end the season with a defeat. He felt sick.

Then an amazing thing happened. As he stood on the field, struggling to hold back his tears, his teammates came and stood with him. They clumsily embraced him, letting him know they forgave his failure. Later Joseph said, "After the kick, I felt empty. But my teammates gave me back my energy." They'd given him more than that; they'd given him new life.

As Christ's disciples, we too will experience failure. But, as the two who met Jesus on the road to Emmaus discovered, failure will not have the final word, for Christ calls us to new life, even in the midst of failure.

Dear God, help me to witness through my failures to the new life available in Jesus Christ. Amen.

OCTOBER 16 CONTROLLING YOUR ANGER

Love is patient; love is kind; love is not envious or boastful or arrogant or rude. It does not insist on its own way; it is not irritable or resentful; it does not rejoice in wrongdoing, but rejoices in the truth. It bears all things, believes all things, hopes all things, endures all things.
—1 Corinthians 13:4-7 (NRSV)

A high school driving instructor was teaching two students to drive when another vehicle cut them off. The instructor ordered the student driver to chase the culprit. When the other driver stopped, the instructor punched him. The other driver then sped off. The instructor again ordered the student to pursue the car. The chase was finally stopped when the student was pulled over for speeding. As the instructor was being ticketed, the other driver drove up and told the police what had happened. The instructor was charged with assault.

Fortunately, most drivers never follow the instructor's example, allowing their anger to lead to "road rage." Unfortunately, at one time or another, most drivers do yell or shake their fists at another driver, thinking they're free to act however they want within the confines of their cars. The truth is, as Christians, we are called to remember our faith and control our anger at all times and in all places.

In 1 Corinthians, Paul describes the constraining power of love. Love gives us power over our anger and the patience we need to be a witness for Christ—wherever we may be.

Dear Lord, make me slow to anger today so that I may witness to your love in all I do. Amen.

CONTROLLING YOUR TONGUE

The tongue is a small member, yet it boasts of great exploits. How great a forest is set ablaze by a small fire! And the tongue is a fire.
—James 3:5-6a

The Oxford American Dictionary defines *gossip* as "casual talk, especially about someone else." It's an activity most of us, especially teens, are quite proficient at! Jeffrey Parker, a University of Michigan psychology professor, found that adolescents talk with friends an average of eighteen times an hour, with gossip taking up as much as half their talking time (*Psychology Today* [July–August 1996]: 44). Parker's research also discovered that because their peers can't trust them, gossips are not particularly popular. It's a risky pastime.

Gossip may seem harmless, but the Bible tells us that the tongue is like a fire and, though small, it can cause great problems. So we must always be careful of what we say. Being a disciple of Christ means saying no to gossip.

Dear God, help me to put out the fire of gossip in my relationships with others. Amen.

TURNING THE OTHER CHEEK

If anyone strikes you on the cheek, offer the other also; and from anyone who takes away your coat do not withhold even your shirt.
—Luke 6:29 (NRSV)

Darryl Williams was a football stand-out with hopes of playing in the NFL. One September evening in 1979, he was playing against rival Charlestown High, a predominantly white school. He had just caught a pass for a touchdown when a shot rang out. In an instant, a sniper's bullet ended Darryl's football career. Paralyzed, he would never play again.

Eleven years later, when he returned to Charlestown High for a speaking engagement, Darryl was asked if he hated whites. "I'm not going to blame every white person because a white man attacked me," he answered. "I can't hate a whole race of people because some are bad. Instead, my dream is to live in a world in which racism doesn't exist anymore" (*The Sporting News*, 11 April 1994, 9).

Darryl defeated hatred by turning the other cheek, just as Jesus taught. Jesus also forgave his enemies, even when they nailed him to a cross. As his disciples, we can do no less.

Dear God, give me the courage to turn the other cheek just as Jesus did. Amen.

OCTOBER 19 FORGIVING YOUR ENEMIES

"You have heard that it was said, 'You shall love your neighbor and hate your enemy.' But I say to you, Love your enemies and pray for those who persecute you."   —Matthew 5:43-44 (NRSV)

Gayle Blount regularly writes the man who murdered her daughter. For years after Catherine's death, Gayle had locked herself in a prison of her own making. Finally, unable to bear her anger, she wrote Catherine's killer.

"I had a beautiful daughter," she wrote. "Her murder saddened me beyond belief." Gayle explained that through prayer she'd been able to forgive:

Though you are guilty, you are still a child of God. The Christ in me sends blessings to the Christ in you.

The death row inmate wrote back thanking her. They now correspond monthly. "I did not want to teach my grandchildren to answer violence with violence," Gayle said (Colman McCarthy, "Mother Forgives, Befriends a Murderer," *National Catholic Reporter,* 25 October 1996, 14).

"Forgive my enemies? the jock who tripped me in the hall? the girl who told lies behind my back? the teacher who embarrassed me? Impossible."

Perhaps forgiving our enemies is impossible—for us, but not for God. As Paul reminds us, "I can do all things through him who strengthens me" (Philippians 4:13 NRSV).

Dear Jesus, help me to forgive my enemies as you forgave yours. Amen.

OCTOBER 20 — LOOKING FOR THE BEST IN OTHERS

Happy are those who find wisdom, and those who get understanding, for her income is better than silver, and her revenue better than gold. —Proverbs 3:13-14 (NRSV)

Hollywood would have us believe that "the good life" is being rich, famous, and attractive. But what does the Bible say? Does it offer a different prescription for happiness?

Yes! Proverbs 3:13-18 basically says that happiness is living "the wise life"—not the good life. Wisdom, it says, is more valuable than silver, gold, and jewels. But what is "the wise life"? Jesus would say "the wise life" is a life of love and compassion. He had the ability to find value in *every* person. The disciples he chose were unpromising, to say the least. Their motley band included fishermen and tax collectors. None of them were rich or famous; yet in the end they changed the world.

Jesus calls us to live "the wise life" by being loving and compassionate, always seeing the best in *every* person.

Dear Jesus, help me to look for the best in each person I meet today. Amen.

OCTOBER 21 — BEING AN ADVOCATE OF RACIAL HARMONY

There is no longer Jew or Greek, there is no longer slave or free, there is no longer male and female; for all of you are one in Christ Jesus.
—Galatians 3:28 (NRSV)

Decades after Rosa Parks refused to yield her seat on a Montgomery bus, America continues to pay a heavy price for racial discord among our population. Today, with the Internet being fertile ground for recruitment of disenchanted teens, hate groups are on the rise.

According to one writer, bigotry in America today is still characteristic of the mainstream of the culture. Many of our children have trouble handling diversity, and their rage gives way to violence.

Jesus reached out to *everyone*, regardless of the color of their skin, their sex, or their religious background. In his sight, each was a child of God. His example of love guided the apostle Paul and the early church; it must guide us today.

Coretta Scott King has said that the fight for freedom is never really over;

each generation has to win it. In other words, *you* are on the front line of the fight against prejudice.

Dear Jesus, give me the wisdom and strength I need to follow your example of loving acceptance. Amen.

HAVING COURAGE AND COMMITMENT

Choose this day whom you will serve; . . . but as for me and my household, we will serve the Lord. —*Joshua 24:15 (NRSV)*

On April 20, 1999, Dylan Klebold and Eric Harris walked into Columbine High School in Littleton, Colorado, and massacred fifteen people. At the height of their rampage, they entered the library. "Who's ready to die?" they yelled. Cassie Bernall, age seventeen, had her Bible open before her. "Do you believe in God?" one of the killers asked. Cassie knew the "safe" answer, but after a moment's hesitation, she answered quietly, "Yes, I do believe in God." Then he shot her (Claire Martin and Janet Bingham, "Cassie Bernall: Girl's Faith a Beacon to Those She Left," *The Denver Post*, 23 April 1999).

Cassie, like Joshua, had come to a moment in her life when she had to make a decision. Was she committed to her faith? Like Christian martyrs before her, Cassie chose to honor God at the cost of her own life.

How about you? Whom will you serve?

Dear God, be with me as I press on in faith, just as Cassie and Joshua did, accepting both the joy and the cost of discipleship. Amen.

LIVING WITHOUT FEAR

God did not give us a spirit of cowardice, but rather a spirit of power and of love and of self-discipline.
—*2 Timothy 1:7 (NRSV)*

At the beginning of every early episode of "The X-Files," these words flashed on the screen: "Trust no one. Fear everything." For many teens, the motto rings true. A recent Ruben Report revealed that a majority of teens worry on a regular basis. Topping their list of fears was anxiety about making poor grades, dying, making mistakes, being popular, and looking good.

As Christians, our motto is "Trust God; fear nothing," for throughout the New Testament the refrain "fear not" rings out again and again. (See Luke 1:13, 30; 2:10; 5:10; 8:50; 12:32; and John 12:15.) Fear and dread have been swallowed up in Christ Jesus.

Trusting in God dispels fear. "God did not give us a spirit of cowardice," writes the author of 2 Timothy. Instead, we are given a "spirit of power and of love and of self-discipline." Hallelujah!

Dear God, help me to face life with courage and power through Jesus Christ. Amen.

CARING FOR CREATION

The LORD God took the man and put him in the garden of Eden to till it and keep it. —Genesis 2:15 (NRSV)

Ever wonder what one individual can do to clean up the world? Well, quite a lot, actually. Take, for example, the eco-crusade of twelve-year-old Will Vinson of Gainesville, Florida. For three years, Will has urged his community to recycle aluminum cans. Armed with the slogan "We love the 3 Rs: reduce, recycle, reuse," Will cajoled his classmates into helping him. Soon the students were recycling hundreds of pounds of cans and donating the proceeds to Head Start. "I knew if I did it," said Will, "the other kids would do it too" ("Litterbugs! This Kid is Out to Clean Up the Town," *Time*, 26 April 1999, 57.)

God placed us in Eden to "till it and keep it." So many have thought this passage grants us permission to pillage the earth's treasures. Actually, it gives us the responsibility of protecting the earth's resources, which are not limitless. Unless we care for creation, we, like Adam and Eve, will be cast out of paradise. But, unlike them, we have nowhere else to go.

Dear Lord, help us to cherish your creation. Amen.

BEING AN ADVOCATE FOR SOCIAL JUSTICE

Then [Jeremiah] said, "Ah, Lord GOD! Truly I do not know how to speak, for I am only a boy." But the LORD said . . . "Do not say, 'I am only a boy'; for you shall go to all to whom I send you, and you shall speak whatever I command you. Do

not be afraid of them, for I am with you to deliver you, says the LORD.*"*
—Jeremiah 1:6-8 (NRSV)

While most teenage girls leaf through *Seventeen,* Maria Perez and Fabiola Tostado, both fifteen, and Nevada Dove, eighteen, read groundwater-safety reports. The girls, dubbed the "Toxic Crusaders," are on an environmental crusade.

Their top priority is the clean-up of Jefferson New Middle School. Their beef? The school was built on contaminated soil. During construction, a dangerous toxin was discovered.

"It's terrifying that kids are going to a school that's contaminated," says Nevada. "They are my sisters and brothers, because they are African American and Hispanic children who may be my neighbors."

The Toxic Crusaders are proud of their advocacy. "We're the new generation," says Nevada. "One day you're going to have to stand up for something you believe in. Why not get an early start?"

Long ago Jeremiah attempted to use his age as an excuse for not speaking out, but God told him, "Do not say, 'I am only a boy.'" As the Toxic Crusaders have proven, nothing is impossible for those who share God's passion for social justice (From "Don't Mess Around with the Toxic Crusaders: Nevada Dove, Fabiola Tistado, Maria Perez," *Time,* 26 April 1999, 56 [1]).

Dear God, give me the courage to speak out on behalf of those who can't. Amen.

 # BEING SEXUALLY RESPONSIBLE

The fruit of the Spirit is . . . self-control. . . . And those who belong to Christ Jesus have crucified the flesh with its passions and desires. —Galatians 5:22-24 (NRSV)

Did you know that 80 percent of teens will have sex before they turn twenty? (Statistic from Tom Schaefer, "Readers Tout the Blessings of Chasitity Before Marriage," Knight-Ridder/Tribune News Service, 20 March 1996). This percentage is surprisingly high in light of all the education youth receive about AIDS and other sexually transmitted diseases. Yet there's hope. A growing number of youth are eliminating sexual risk by choosing to remain virgins until marriage.

A. C. Green, a NBA basketball player and a devout Christian, applauds their self-control. Green remains true to a pledge of abstinence. "I abstain as an adult for the same reasons I did as a teen," he said. "The principle doesn't change. I believe in abstinence before marriage" (David

Whitman, "Was It Good for Us?" *U.S. News and World Report,* 19 May 1997, p. 56).

Jesus taught that the unrestrained pursuit of gratification, either material or sexual, leads to unhappiness. So treasure your body as the "temple of the Holy Spirit" it is (1 Corinthians 6:19). Waiting, though difficult, is worth it.

Dear Lord, give me the self-control I need to wait for true love. Amen.

 # DEALING HONESTLY WITH OTHERS

You shall not steal; you shall not deal falsely; and you shall not lie to one another. —Leviticus 19:11 (NRSV)

"Liar, liar! Pants on fire!" If this childhood ditty is to be believed, then many teens should be smelling smoke! A national survey of American teenagers revealed a disconcerting trend: The number of teens who admit to dishonest behavior has risen significantly in recent years.

Forty-six percent of the teens surveyed said they had shoplifted (up from 39 percent in 1996), 70 percent said they had cheated on an exam (up from 64 percent), and 92 percent said they had lied to their parents (up from 85 percent).

As disciples of Christ, we are called to deal honestly with one another. Though our peers may lie, cheat, and steal, we are called to behave as Jesus would—for our lives are a witness to Christ.

Dear Jesus, lead me in the path of honesty. Amen.

 # BEING A GOOD MONEY STEWARD

No one can serve two masters; for a slave will either hate the one and love the other, or be devoted to the one and despise the other. You cannot serve God and wealth. —Matthew 6:24 (NRSV)

In 1993, a survey on religion and economic values conducted by Princeton University found that 71 percent of Americans agree with this statement: "Being greedy is a sin against God." Yet three out of four of those surveyed rejected the view that it is morally wrong to be wealthy while others starve.

This study points to our uneasiness with money. In contrast, Jesus did not hesitate to discuss wealth's corrupting influence. In fact, he spoke five times more about money than he did about prayer.

In Matthew 6:24, Jesus draws the battle line when he declares, "You cannot serve God and wealth." By contrasting loyalty to God with loyalty to wealth, Jesus personifies money's influence in our lives—giving it the spiritual authority of a rival god. "Are you using money," Jesus asks us, "or is money using you?"

Jesus knew that all that glitters is not gold. In the words of an African proverb, "Being well-dressed does not prevent us from being poor."

Dear Lord, help me to use my money wisely on behalf of those in need. Amen.

OCTOBER 29 OBEYING THE WILL OF GOD

Then he [Jesus] said to them, "I am deeply grieved, even to death; remain here and stay awake with me." And going a little farther, he threw himself on the ground and prayed, "My Father, if it is possible, let this cup pass from me; yet not what I want but what you want."
—Matthew 26:38-39 (NRSV)

Jesus has eaten what he knows is to be his last meal. Events are moving swiftly and treason is afoot. He retires with his disciples to the garden called Gethsemane. After asking his disciples to wait for him, he goes to pray.

The portrayal of Jesus in Gethsemane is not the conquering Messiah, the victorious Christ. Instead, the Jesus in the garden is a lonely, very ordinary man wracked with fear. He doesn't want to suffer. He wants to live as we all want to live. He is uncertain, scared, and desperate.

But then, in the ultimate moment of self-surrender, he empties himself and openly embraces God's will. "My Father," he says, "if it is possible, let this cup pass from me; yet not what I want but what you want."

Jesus set an example for us—an example of a life of obedience, a life empowered by an abiding trust in God.

Dear Lord, help me to live my life obedient to your Word. Amen.

OCTOBER 30
OBEYING THE TEN COMMANDMENTS

Moses convened all Israel, and said to them: Hear, O Israel, the statutes and ordinances that I am addressing to you today; you shall learn them and observe them diligently. —Deuteronomy 5:1 (NRSV)

When 1,200 people were asked to name the Ten Commandments in a survey conducted several years ago, most could name no more than two, and, as essayist Cullen Murphy writes, "They weren't too happy about some of the others when they were told about them" (*U.S. News and World Report,* 18 November 1996, 6).

Why doesn't our society pay God's law more heed? The answer lies in our culture. We live in an age in which individualism is our creed. So to many people, the Ten Commandments—which provide a framework for community life lived under the sovereignty of God—simply do not seem relevant any longer. Some have even suggested we change their name to a more palatable "Ten Suggestions."

God calls us into covenant. The Ten Commandments challenge our willingness to be obedient, to denounce other gods, to practice justice, and to embrace loyalty to a liberating faith. As disciples of Christ, we are called to incorporate God's law into our community life—before it's too late. Will you do your part?

Dear Lord, help me to obey your commandments and be an example for others. Amen.

OCTOBER 31
STUDYING THE WORD OF GOD

From childhood you have known the sacred writings that are able to instruct you for salvation through faith in Jesus Christ. All scripture is inspired by God and is useful for teaching, for reproof, for correction, and for training in righteousness, so that everyone who belongs to God may be proficient, equipped for every good work. —2 Timothy 3:15-17

Question: Who preached the Sermon on the Mount? If you answered "Jesus," then congratulations! In a survey of professing Christians conducted by pollster George Gallup several years ago, only half answered this question correctly. According to Gallup, this startling piece of collective ignorance is evidence that biblical illiteracy has reached an all time high. "Americans say they believe in the Ten Commandments," he says, "but they can't name them. And some Christians who are in church on Easter don't know what they are commemorating" (Karen R. Long, "Bible Knowledge at Record Low," *National Catholic Reporter,* 15 July 1994, 9).

A disciple of Jesus Christ is grounded in the Bible, for without its witness, we wouldn't know the saving Word of Jesus Christ. Within its ancient pages lies the power to transform the world. Martin Luther once said of scripture: "Poor and mean are the swaddling clothes but dear is the treasure which lies within." Take time today to look in the Book. It's a habit that can change your life!

Dear God, thank you for giving me the guidance of your Holy Word. Amen.

LESSONS IN LOVE
FROM A
YELLOW LAB

Matthew D. Stultz

LESSONS IN LOVE FROM A YELLOW LAB

Matthew D. Stultz

A GIFT FROM GOD

How many are your works, O Lord! In wisdom you made them all; the earth is full of your creatures. —Psalm 104:24

Have you ever been sad or lonely, and giving your dog a hug or letting your cat snuggle up in your lap helped to make things better? How many times has the friendly face of your dog or the welcoming rub of your cat made you smile? And how can you stay mad when there's a puppy or kitten nipping at your heels?

Pets are a gift from God. In his infinite wisdom, God gave us pets to be our special companions. They accept us, love us, comfort us, and increase our joy. Funny, but God does all those things too. Maybe that's why we love our pets so much: They remind us of God's love.

This month I will share some of the "lessons" I've learned from my dog, Hercules. Even if you don't have a pet, you can appreciate these reminders of God's unconditional and abiding love.

Dear God, thank you for all the creatures of this world, especially the animals you have provided to be our special companions. Help me to see each living creature as a wise and wonderful gift from you. Amen.

GOD IS IN CONTROL

"For I know the plans I have for you," declares the Lord, "plans to prosper you and not to harm you, plans to give you hope and a future." —Jeremiah 29:11

I decided to get a puppy two years ago. I had decided on a female black lab, but when I came back, only yellow ones were left. I ended up picking a large male who pushed his way into the food dish to eat. It turns out that Hercules—Herc, for short—was the pick of the litter.

We try and try to plan our lives the best we can. At times we even think we know better than God. I don't know what would have happened if I had gotten the little black dog. All I know is that I like the way it worked out.

The same thing holds true for every aspect of my life. Even when I can't make sense of things at first, I eventually see that God is working for good in my life; and for that I am eternally grateful.

Almighty God, thank you for the way you work things out in my life. When I can't see the forest for the trees, I'm glad you are always there seeing the big picture. Amen.

PROBLEMS ADJUSTING

Come to me, all you who are weary and burdened, and I will give you rest.

—Matthew 11:28

The first night I brought Hercules home, he was really scared. I put him in a large box with a shredded blanket and placed the box next to my bed. Halfway through the night, I heard a soft whimpering. I took him outside— nothing. I tried everything I could think of, and still he would not go to sleep. Finally, I picked him up, sat down in my recliner, and slowly rocked him. When I looked down at the little guy, he was fast asleep. I guess all he needed was to feel my love and know he was safe.

The cure for our own difficult times is the simple love of God. Whether you're adjusting to a new school or to life without a close friend or loved one, God understands what you're going through and how hard it is. Just relax; he'll take care of you.

God, let me turn to you with my fears. Let the simplicity of your love overpower my anxiety. And let me truly find rest in you. Amen.

SIN AND GRACE

*But where sin increased, grace increased all the more, so that,
just as sin reigned in death, so also grace might reign through
righteousness to bring eternal life through Jesus Christ our Lord.*
—Romans 5:20b-21

When Hercules was five-and-a-half-weeks old, he caught a small field
mouse. I tried everything I could think of to make him drop it. I tried to
force his jaws open and only felt sharp puppy teeth. Eventually, I offered
him a puppy treat, and he spit out the mouse.

I knew that letting Hercules keep the mouse in his mouth would only
make him sick. He had no clue that the mouse could hurt him. He just
wanted to have something to play with.

Sin is like that in our lives. God tries and tries to get us to understand the
danger we are in, but we clench our jaws and hang on for a fight. Often our
sharp infant teeth cut as God tries to take the sin out of our lives. If we
would just give up the struggle, we could find the true reward in God's
grace.

**Lord, help me understand the danger of sin and find healing
and peace in your mercy and forgiveness. Amen.**

FACING
YOUR FEARS

*He said, "Do not fear, greatly beloved, you are safe. Be strong
and courageous!"* —Daniel 10:19a (NRSV)

It was Hercules' first summer. He had seen me and my wife splashing in
the pool, and he wanted in on the fun. Taking one step off the side, he fell
face first into the water. He came up, found his way to the steps, and finally
made it to the yard—panting and shaking the water off. We haven't been
able to keep him out of the water since!

Hercules knew that we were there and wouldn't let anything hurt him.
Because he trusted us, he fearlessly jumped into the pool. God wants us to
trust him like that. He wants us to experience life and grow. Life can be
really scary at times, but part of dealing with fear is "jumping in" and going
on. Following God doesn't mean our fears go away. It simply means we are
given the courage and strength to face our fears.

**Give me courage, O Lord. Help me to face my fears, finding my
strength in your love. Amen.**

TURN THE OTHER CHEEK

But I say to you, Do not resist an evildoer. But if anyone strikes you on the right cheek, turn the other also.
—*Matthew 5:39 (NRSV)*

When Hercules was a puppy, my friend Justin loved to blow on his face. Herc didn't like it much, and he would nip at the air. One time Justin got a little too close, and Herc nipped him on the lip. I know Herc just wanted to get away, but I punished him because I didn't want him to be a dog that bites. Hercules didn't understand, but he learned not to bite! Since then, he has learned to tolerate kids pulling on his tail and tugging on his ears—without even a growl.

Turning the other cheek means not seeking revenge. It is especially important to turn the other cheek at school, where the rumor networks are always working overtime. If someone is spreading rumors about you, it doesn't help to try to hurt that person in some way. It only makes you look bad. Be strong. Don't tarnish your good reputation. Trust me: People who spread rumors eventually find themselves without friends.

God, help me to stand firm on your Word and not seek revenge. Amen.

GROWING UP

When I was a child, I talked like a child, I thought like a child, I reasoned like a child. When I became [an adult], I put childish ways behind me.
—*1 Corinthians 13:11*

It took Hercules longer to be completely house broken than I had hoped. For a while, I was really worried about it. I even thought that something might be wrong. After a little more time, he finally caught on. I was relieved, but I felt bad for having worried about it so much.

Growing up isn't easy for any of us—puppies or people! We want to grow up, drive a car, and go out on dates, leaving childhood behind. On the other hand, we don't want to give up the security of being a child, of always being protected.

Growing up doesn't change how God protects us, though. His role in guiding us only becomes more important as we mature. To grow up properly, we have to listen to God's guidance, leave childhood behind, and embrace being a *child of God*—no matter how old we get.

Father God, thank you for the eternal youth I have because of you. I know I will grow old; but with your Spirit, I know my heart will stay young. Help me with the struggles of growing up, and guide me into adulthood. Amen.

COMFORTING OTHERS

For the Lamb at the center of the throne will be their shepherd; he will lead them to springs of living water. And God will wipe away every tear from their eyes. —*Revelation 7:17*

Sometimes I think that Herc knows my moods better than I do. It never fails that when I am sad, he comes to me and lays his head on my lap, looking up with sympathetic eyes. It always makes me feel better knowing that he is there. Being a dog, he never tries to say the "right thing." He's just there for me and wants me to remember that.

Have you ever tried to comfort someone who has just lost a loved one or received very bad news? Words are never enough, are they? God wants us to be there for others when they are sad, and sometimes the best words of comfort are spoken in silence. There are no words of comfort that can take pain away. Only God can heal a broken heart. Just being there for someone is a reminder of God's love.

God, let me remember that you alone can heal the pain of the heart. May I be there for others to remind them of your love. Amen.

TRUE FRIENDSHIP

A friend loves at all times. —*Proverbs 17:17a*

My parents have a little white Cockapoo named Audrey. It would take about twenty-eight of her to make one Hercules. At first we were really worried that Herc might hurt Audrey. As it turns out, the two are best friends. They love playing tug together. Herc just lies there and lets Audrey pull. Sure, there is an occasional growl between them, but they always end up happy with each other.

There is nothing like friendship. Sometimes, though, it can be hard to tell who your *true* friends are. Many times people pretend to be our friends and then say cruel things behind our backs. That isn't true friendship. True friends are able to get over petty disagreements and move on. True friends love each other at *all* times, even when it isn't easy.

Love your friends at all times. If they're true friends, you'll find they'll do the same.

Father, thank you for my friends. Teach us not to take one another for granted. Help us to listen to one another and to love one another at all times. Amen.

TURNING ENEMIES INTO FRIENDS

You have heard that it was said, "Love your neighbor and hate your enemy." But I tell you: Love your enemies and pray for those who persecute you. —Matthew 5:43-44

My sister has a dog named Sascha who doesn't like Hercules very much. Each time Herc sees Sascha, he tries to be friendly. She only growls at him—sometimes even snapping. This doesn't discourage Herc very much. He never growls back or becomes upset. He never stops trying. I suppose he thinks she will give in one day and be his friend.

God doesn't want us to stop trying with others, either. When people make life difficult for us, we should not respond in anger. God wants us to be kind. After all, most people act cruel only because they have been mistreated or hurt in the past.

We seldom take the time to understand someone before we decide that we don't like that person. Just remember: A little love goes a long way. And a little understanding just might turn an enemy into a friend.

Dear God, help me to reach out to others, even if I don't like them very much. And when others are unkind to me, remind me to pray for them so that your love may heal their anger. Amen.

NEVER ALONE

"Then you will say in your heart, 'Who bore me these? I was bereaved and barren; I was exiled and rejected. . . . I was left all alone.' " —Isaiah 49:21

It was the first time we had left Hercules alone for a long time. We made arrangements for my sister to come over and let him out. The only snag in the plan was that we neglected to give her a key to the house! We came home to find Herc's big, brown eyes looking at us as if to say, "Did you forget me?"

We all know what it's like to feel lonely and sad. But no one knows it better than Jesus. In the last hours of his life on this earth, his friends turned their backs on him and deserted him when he needed them most. So the next time you feel like no one understands what you are going through, just remember Jesus. Remember he is there for you, and you are never alone.

Lord, stay with me. Help me to remember how lonely you felt the night before you were crucified and how much you suffered for me. I know you are with me, especially when no one else is. Thank you for your faithfulness. Amen.

GOD'S PATIENT GRACE

"Listen! I am standing at the door, knocking; if you hear my voice and open the door, I will come in to you and eat with you, and you with me." —Revelation 3:20 (NRSV)

Every morning Hercules wakes up before my wife and I do. He goes from side to side of the bed, trying to figure out who will be taking him outside. He even jumps up between us and looks for any signs of life. If there is no movement, then he simply lies down. Herc doesn't move until we do. Finally, when one of us sits up, he becomes excited and literally hops around until we take him out. But until that time, he is perfectly patient.

God is waiting—waiting for our response to a question asked before we were even born. "Will you follow me?" he asks, giving us a lifetime to answer. There are many times we could answer, but he doesn't want us to rush; he only wants us to be sincere. "Here I am!" he says. "When will you open that door?"

Lord Jesus, I know you are waiting for my answer—and you want it to come from my heart. Help me to understand the things that confuse me—the things that scare me about truly following you. Amen.

GOOD STEWARDSHIP

The LORD God took the man and put him in the Garden of Eden to work it and take care of it. —Genesis 2:15

When Hercules needs to go outside, he sits by the door. Sometimes I get really busy and don't see him sitting there. One of his ways of getting back at me is pooping in the front room. He has only done this a couple of times, but that's enough! If I'd just taken the time to let him out, those accidents never would have happened.

We have a duty to take care of creation, yet we can see trash on almost every stretch of highway. Usually, we don't take time to stop to pick up and throw away a paper cup or an aluminum can, thinking that someone else will do it. If this sounds more like an environmental commercial than a devotional, remember that we are the stewards of creation. Stewardship simply means "to take care of." So, if we don't do our part to take care of the planet, we shouldn't be surprised when we find poop in the front room.

God, thank you for your gift of creation. Help us to take care of this precious gift by taking the initiative to pitch in and work together. Amen.

NOVEMBER 14 — PRAISE THE LORD!

Let everything that has breath praise the LORD. —Psalm 150:6

Hercules gets excited easily. Every night as we go to bed, he follows us and jumps onto the bed. If he gets even the slightest pat on the head, he spins around in circles. All the blankets twist into a giant ball, and he sits there, panting. I suppose he's just happy to be with us, wanting us to know that he loves us.

We often hear about how much God loves us. It's the overwhelming theme of the gospels. But what about how much we love God? Shouldn't we be anxious to let God know we love him? That's what the word *praise* really means. When we say, "Praise the Lord," we're really saying, "Thank you, God!"

The next time you find yourself in a good mood, filled with joy, just look toward heaven and say, "Praise the Lord!"

God, I love you. Today I join the rest of creation in praising you. Open my eyes to see you all around me. Amen.

NOVEMBER 15 — JOY

Shout for joy to the LORD, all the earth. —Psalm 98:4a

Every once in a while, Hercules will get up from a nap, take a big stretch, and then shoot up and down the house at warp speed.

The only thing we can do is watch in amazement. I can't explain it. My wife and I exercise Herc on a daily basis, so we can rule out the need for exercise. The look on his face and the manner of his activity lead me to think there is a simple reason for it—he's happy.

When was the last time you felt such joy you couldn't help jumping up and down, running down the hallway, or shouting out loud? The joy of the Lord is always a reason for us to celebrate. Maybe we shouldn't show it by running through the house at warp speed, but we can show it by sharing spontaneous smiles and words of praise. Try it today!

Lord, help me to claim my joy and freely praise you for the blessings you give me each and every day. Amen.

 ## GOD KNOWS YOUR HEART

Nothing in all creation is hidden from God's sight. Everything is uncovered and laid bare before the eyes of him to whom we must give account. —Hebrews 4:13

My wife's parents have a Pomeranian named Dusty. Once when we were visiting, Hercules decided to be friendly and share his three-pound, chewing bone with Dusty. When Herc dropped the bone, it hit Dusty on the head, leaving quite a lump. We didn't scold Herc, because we knew he didn't mean to hurt Dusty. Dusty, on the other hand, didn't realize that it was an accident, and she was really mad. Hercules instantly laid his ears back, trying to say he was sorry.

Have you ever seen someone "get away with something"? You think it just isn't fair because the person doesn't get in trouble. Well, just as we knew that Herc didn't mean to hurt Dusty, God knows everyone's heart— and it is up to God alone to judge. Maybe that's why Jesus told us to be more concerned about the log in our own eye than we are about the speck in our neighbor's eye (Matthew 7:3). Remember, *nothing* is hidden from God.

Almighty God, I know you know my heart. Help me to hold more love in my heart and grow more like Jesus every day. Amen.

IDOLS

They worshiped their idols, which became a snare to them.
—Psalm 106:36

Herc's favorite toy is a tennis ball. You hardly ever see him without it; he's either chewing on it or placing it on the nearest lap. Even when he sleeps, the ball is never far away.

A tennis ball is a harmless toy, right? Well, one of his favorite games is to throw the ball under the couch and try to get it. While playing this game once, Hercules not only managed to get the ball stuck under the couch; *he* became wedged under the couch too. After I stopped laughing, I helped him out. Sometimes something that seems harmless can get you into trouble after all.

We all have our idols—things that keep God from being the number one priority in our lives. For some, it's money; for others, it's popularity. Anything that takes our attention away from God is an idol. When we lose our focus on God, we lose our way. But if we focus on God, then everything else just falls into place.

God, help me to make you my number one priority and let everything else just fall into place. Amen.

JUST ASK

So I say to you: Ask and it will be given to you; seek and you will find; knock and the door will be opened to you. —Luke 11:9

One day Hercules locked himself in the guest bedroom. He went into the room to get his toy, and the door shut behind him. I had no idea he was even in there. Eventually, I noticed the door was closed. When I opened it, I found Herc lying there. He looked up, picked up his toy, and quietly walked into the living room. If he had just let me know he was trapped, I would have let him out sooner!

In life, we often get ourselves trapped in circumstances we can't escape. We go chasing our dreams or desires only to find the door closing behind us. All we need to do is ask God to open the door—to give us the guidance we need to avoid any more traps—yet we remain silent, alone in the dark. One word is all it would take to get our freedom back.

Lord, give me the strength to call out to you when I am trapped. I believe you will open the door if I will only ask. Thank you for your faithfulness. Amen.

HABITS

"Watch out for false prophets. They come to you in sheep's cloth-ing, but inwardly they are ferocious wolves. By their fruit you will recognize them." —Matthew 7:15-16

Hercules loves fast food. Whenever he's in the car with me at the drive-thru and he hears the garbled, "Please drive around," he begins to drool. I always get him a plain hamburger, his favorite. One time, just as we were pulling around, the person in the window said, "Hi, Hercules!" I didn't real-ize we had been going there so much!

Others know us by our habits—what we say, what we eat, where and how we choose to spend our time. In other words, they know us by the "fruit" we bear in our lives. Wherever we are and whatever we're doing, others are watching us. When Jesus warned his disciples about false teachers, he said, "You will know these people by what they do." We need to remember that others can learn about God through our actions as well as our words. In fact, our actions speak more loudly than our words. Our habits should show others how much we love God.

God, help me to realize that my actions affect others, that my life can be a witness to your glory, and that even my mistakes can be a tribute to you. Amen.

PLAYING HIDE AND SEEK

Who can hide in secret places so that I cannot see them? says the LORD. Do I not fill heaven and earth? says the LORD.
—Jeremiah 23:23 (NRSV)

I walked quietly through the house, into the spare bedroom, and behind the bed where I crouched down and hid. He heard me. I could hear him walking quickly through the house, searching. He was close, but I had fooled him. Just as I smiled a smile of celebration, I looked up. There was Herc on the bed, looking down at me! So much for playing hide and seek with a dog.

If you think hiding from a dog is hard to do, just read the book of Jonah. He tried to hide from God but finally realized it was impossible. I've known people who think they can hide from God. They even try to "hide" in church, thinking, "If I just pretend I'm a Christian, then maybe God won't expect more from my life." Sound familiar?

Just as you can't physically hide from God, so also you can't hide who you are from God. God sees you and loves you just as you are. Remember, God created you in his own image.

Father, thank you for your careful watch over me. Help me remember how much you love me just as I am. Amen.

PURE EQUALITY

There is no longer Jew or Greek, there is no longer slave or free, there is no longer male and female; for all of you are one in Christ Jesus. —Galatians 3:28 (NRSV)

Hercules is not registered by the American Kennel Club. Actually, his mom is a Golden Retriever and his dad is a Black Labrador. So, I call Herc a Golden Lab. I always wanted an AKC dog, just for the name. But now that I have him, I really don't care about the title. I love him simply because he's mine.

We are all different. Most of us are a blend of peoples and cultures. Take me, for example. I'm part German and part Irish. I love my family and my heritage, but those things don't define *who I am.* My faith in Christ defines who I am—I am a Christian. And Christ loves me simply because I'm his.

That is what Paul is writing about in today's passage: equality. As Christians, no matter where we come from, we are all equal in Christ.

God, thank you for creating us equal. Help us to celebrate our diversity in culture and embrace our equality in Christ. Amen.

BE STILL AND TRUST

Be still, and know that I am God! —Psalm 46:10a

We all love a good night's sleep. But if our sleep isn't peaceful, it isn't restful. Every night when Hercules finally lies down, he lets out a simple sigh. That's when I know he's ready for sleep. I think he sighs because he is at peace. There isn't anything else to do. The day is over, and it's time for rest.

I wish I could always follow my dog's example. There are nights when thoughts are racing through my mind and sleep doesn't come very easily. I don't know why I worry so much. Worries are just life events we don't think God can handle. Think about it: If we really thought God could handle a problem, then we wouldn't worry about it.

When we go to bed at night, we need to learn to take a deep breath, let it out, and be still, putting all our trust in God.

Almighty God, help me to be still and know your strength. Teach me to let go of my worries, trust you completely, and find your peace. Amen.

SOMETIMES WE JUST NEED HELP

He said to the paralyzed man, "I tell you, get up, take your mat and go home." Immediately he stood up in front of them, took what he had been lying on and went home praising God. Everyone was amazed and gave praise to God. They were filled with awe and said, "We have seen remarkable things today."　　　　　　　　　　　　　　　　*—Luke 5:24b-26*

I used to smoke. I'm not proud of it, but I did. I tried to quit many times. Once, I came home from work to find all my cigarettes broken on the floor. Hercules had torn open a package and had busted each individual cigarette. I didn't have any more money to feed my habit, so I just wound up quitting. Thanks, Herc!

The paralyzed man was just sitting there. That was all that he could do until he met Jesus. Then God gave him the opportunity he needed to get on with his life. That's what God does—gives opportunities for our redemption.

Perhaps smoking or something even more serious is distracting you from God's message. Just like my smoking was affecting Hercules (or he wouldn't have destroyed my cigarettes!), so also our sin affects our loved ones as well as ourselves. We need to be open to the opportunities God gives us for healing.

Almighty God, open my eyes to the opportunities you give me for healing, for repentance. May these opportunities lead me closer to you. Amen.

GIVING THANKS

Be joyful always; pray continually; give thanks in all circumstances, for this is God's will for you in Christ Jesus.　　　　　　　　　　　　　　　　*—1 Thessalonians 5:16-18*

Hercules is always saying "thank you." Each day that I fill up his food dispenser and water dish, he comes to me and lays his head on my lap just to say "thank you." The other day I filled up his water dish and then lay down on the couch to take a nap. Herc woke me up to say "thank you" by putting his slimy face on my cheek. I wiped off my face and said, "You're welcome."

Paul says we are to "give thanks in all circumstances." In other words, "look for the good in all things." Even on the worst day, something good happens—or something bad doesn't happen! Paul also says we are to "pray continually." That might be difficult to do if we think prayer is words and sentences only—whether spoken or unspoken. We need to remember that prayer is also having a thankful heart—one that beats continually in thanksgiving to God.

Thank you, God, for the blessings you place in my life. Help me to give thanks to you always by letting a thankful pulse of prayer beat continually in my heart. Amen.

VANITY

Vanity of vanities, says the Teacher, vanity of vanities! All is vanity. —*Ecclesiastes 1:2 (NRSV)*

I think Hercules is vain. Every chance he gets, he looks in the mirror. He just sits there and stares. At first I thought that *he* thought he was seeing another dog. So one time I waved my hand behind his head to see if he would look at the reflection. Instead, he turned and looked at my hand! Spooky. He knew he was looking at a reflection—which is why I think he's vain.

Why are we so concerned with our looks? When this life comes to an end, do you think it will matter to God what kind of jeans you wore or if you smelled like peaches or had designer shoes? Sure, it's important to feel good about yourself, as long as you don't get caught up in your image. But it's even more important to be concerned about being a good person and caring for others. Remember, it's your heart that matters.

God, thank you for the beauty you have created in me. Let me remember that you love me and think I am special. Help me to feel that way too. Amen.

WAITING FOR GOD

Lead me in your truth, and teach me, for you are the God of my salvation; for you I wait all day long. —*Psalm 25:5 (NRSV)*

Every time I come home, Hercules is sitting by the door waiting for me. No matter what kind of day it has been, good or bad, he is there waiting for me. Seeing that tail wagging for me always puts a smile on my face. It's nice to know I am loved.

We don't usually wait for God. We say our prayers, list our wants, and move on. When was the last time you just sat and waited for God—simply because you love him? With our busy schedules, it's difficult to find time to wait and listen for God. But, after all, God is the source of our salvation. That alone merits sitting and waiting for the rest of our lives. A few minutes a day shouldn't be too hard.

Lord, help me to make time for you and wait for you with anxious patience so that I may hear your guidance. Amen.

BE READY!

Be on guard! Be alert! You do not know when that time will come. It's like a man going away: He leaves his house and puts his servants in charge, each with his assigned task, and tells the one at the door to keep watch. . . . If he comes suddenly, do not let him find you sleeping. —Mark 13:33-34, 36

It's 5:00 A.M., and I hear a noise. I know it's a mouse, so I rally the troops. I grab a flashlight, hand my wife a broom, and call the dog. We go into the kitchen, and I think I hear it in the closet. I open the door, knowing that Herc is going to pounce. A gray streak shoots between Herc's legs and scurries under the fridge. Herc looks up at me as if to say, "Come on! I'm not even awake yet!"

No one knows when Jesus will come back. The key is to be ready always—to be ready *now*. How do we get ready? If we follow the Word and do our best to grow as Christians, then we'll be ready. Christ knows that none of us is perfect; what he wants is our perfect *effort*.

Lord Jesus, help me to be ready. Transform my heart and mind so that I may grow closer to you and be prepared for your return. Amen.

EXPECT THE UNEXPECTED

I came that they may have life, and have it abundantly. —John 10:10b (NRSV)

We used to live in the middle of nowhere. Every night Hercules and I would go for a short walk. I let him track rabbits simply because of the joy it brought him. The chases always ended with a little white tail hopping down the trail.

One night Herc picked up a strong scent. Suddenly a large buck tore through the brush, passed in front of us, and pranced through the forest. Herc looked up at me as if to say, "That's it; I quit! No more rabbit chasing for me!"

Jesus wants us to live each day to its fullest. One way we do this is by learning to expect the unexpected. We need to be careful not to get so caught up in our own little worlds that we're ready to throw up our hands and quit when things don't go as we planned. After all, life is full of surprises, and with God's help, we can learn to see those surprises as opportunities rather than disappointments or setbacks.

Don't let life become a dull routine; live creatively. Expect the unexpected. Make the most of every day, starting now!

Lord, teach me to expect the unexpected and live each day to the fullest. Amen.

FLAWS

We all stumble in many ways. —James 3:2a

Drool is Herc's biggest flaw. I can be eating a sandwich or even a potato chip, and the "water works" are turned on. So why not get rid of him if it bothers me? Well, drooling *is* gross, but I'm not going to get rid of Herc for something that just annoys me, especially when there are so many good things about him. I just make sure that I have an extra napkin to take care of the problem.

We all have flaws. Each of us has at least one thing we struggle with. Maybe it's our gossiping or our vocabulary that causes us to stumble. Regardless, we should never give up on doing better. We should never say, "Well, I just can't get it right, so why bother." We may not be able to overcome our flaws, but God can. Remember, "All things are possible with God" (Mark 10:27b).

God, I know I'm not perfect. Please help me do my best to be more like Jesus. Amen.

NOVEMBER 30

TOGETHER FOREVER

And surely I am with you always, to the very end of the age.
—Matthew 28:20b

Do you ever wonder if dogs—or cats or any other pets—go to heaven? I do. And although I don't know the answer, I do know that the Bible tells us there will be many creatures in heaven: "Then I heard every creature in heaven and on earth and under the earth and in the sea, and all that is in them, singing: 'To him who sits upon the throne and to the Lamb be blessing and honor and glory and might, for ever and ever!' " (Revelation 5:13 RSV). Regardless of what heaven will be like and who we will see there, the best part is that we'll be with God forever—"to the very end of the age."

There's no harm in picturing heaven. In fact, as we close our journey together this month, I'd like to share a poem I've written about my own picture of heaven:

> The golden path winds to the towering falls.
> Clouds envelop the crystalline walls.
> The air is filled with angelic song
> At the gate I am greeted by all friends since gone;
> My family, my friends, all those I have missed.
> The tears are now streaming from joy and from bliss.
> But there in the front is a friend dear to me.
> He's been sitting there waiting for me patiently.
> My heart is full and my soul is at peace.
> I'm reunited with all, including my Hercules.

Gentle Father, thank you for your presence in my life; thank you for all those who mean so much to me, especially my animal friends; and thank you that, because of Jesus, "good-bye" is not forever. Amen.

KEYS TO
A HAPPY
LIFE

Al and Sharon Meeds

KEYS TO A HAPPY LIFE

Al and Sharon Meeds

BE HAPPY "JUST BECAUSE"

*Let the heavens rejoice, let the earth be glad; let them say
among the nations, "The LORD reigns!" Let the sea resound, and
all that is in it; let the fields be jubilant, and everything in them!*
— 1 Chronicles 16:31-32

Sometimes you've just gotta be happy. Even when things aren't going quite like you planned and life seems a bit rougher than usual, sometimes you've just gotta be happy! On those days when there's no particular reason to rejoice, just think of our great God and you will find a reason. See the word pictures in this Scripture passage—the seas, resounding and praising God; the fields, jubilant—and you can't help but be happy. If the very planet we are on can praise God, we can surely find some reason to be happy and thankful. And even if you can't find a reason, sometimes you just gotta be happy anyway!

Help me to be happy today, God, just because. Amen.

FIND WORK YOU LOVE TO DO

*I know that there is nothing better for them than to be happy
and enjoy themselves as long as they live; moreover, it is God's
gift that all should eat and drink and take pleasure in all their toil.*
—Ecclesiastes 3:12-13 (NRSV)

Toil, a gift of God? Strangely, this can be true. Our line of work is youth ministry; and although this work occupies a lot of our time, it brings us much happiness and satisfaction. We truly believe that the opportunity to minister to young people is a great gift from God, and we are thankful for it. It's true that our work also brings us stress and disappointment at times; but we have found that, with God's help, there's nothing we can't handle.

Life is a long road, and if you can do the things you love to do while serving the God you love, your trek will be a happy one.

Hey, God, please help me to find the work I love and to love the work I do. Amen.

FOLLOW GOD

For to the one who pleases him God gives wisdom and knowledge and joy; but to the sinner he gives the work of gathering and heaping, only to give to one who pleases God.
—*Ecclesiastes 2:26 (NRSV)*

How's that again? If I please God, I get the good stuff; and those who don't please God get to work for nothing. Maybe I've been looking for happiness in all the wrong places. Maybe following God is the true road to a happy life, with a little knowledge and wisdom thrown in for good measure. I can live with that. I'm not lazy or anything, but it seems that pleasing God is easier than wasting my life working for things that only will be taken away. I'll only be young once, but I can be happy for a lifetime by pleasing God.

God, please give me the wisdom to know what is pleasing to you so that I can live happily ever after. Amen.

PRAY OFTEN AND SING FOR JOY

Are any among you suffering? They should pray. Are any cheerful? They should sing songs of praise.   —*James 5:13 (NRSV)*

Is life really that simple? If you're in trouble, pray. If you're happy, sing. Sounds just too easy. And don't I need to have some special prayer book or some special place to pray? Don't I need to have a special voice to sing?

Life *can* be simple when you serve God. Of course, if you pray when you're *not* in trouble, you'll have it down pat when you call for help; and there are other "frequent pray-er" benefits as well. Making a joyful noise to our God is another wonderful tradition because God hears the music from our hearts, not from our mouths.

Hello, God. Help me to pray more often and remind me to sing for joy! Amen.

DECEMBER 5 — REJOICE ALWAYS, EVEN WHEN IT RAINS

Be glad, O people of Zion, rejoice in the LORD your God, for he has given you the autumn rains in righteousness. He sends you abundant showers, both autumn and spring rains. —Joel 2:23

We live in the Seattle area, where rain is pretty normal. Sometimes we get really tired of gray skies and wet feet. It can be hard to rejoice when your whole world is shades of gray. Thinking of the rain as a gift from God, or as a symbol of righteousness, helps a little. But for those of us who live in rainy climates, the sun just seems to make it easier to praise God; for desert dwellers, it's the rain.

Wherever we may live and whatever may be going on in our lives, God always provides a way for us to rejoice and worship him. For starters, we can rejoice in the knowledge that God is in control of the rain as well as the sun.

God, please be my umbrella when the showers get in the way of my rejoicing. Amen.

DECEMBER 6 — BELIEVE THE PROMISES OF GOD

Then maidens will dance and be glad, young men and old as well. I will turn their mourning into gladness; I will give them comfort and joy instead of sorrow. —Jeremiah 31:13

Sometimes it's really hard to be happy. Sometimes bad things do happen to us and to those we love. Often we don't understand why. The only things we can lean on in those situations are the promises of God. Somehow, some way, God will come through for us. Our sorrow and our mourning will be turned into gladness and dancing. How? However God chooses. Why? Because God loves us and cares for us. This is the miracle of our God—the ability to change bad into good, water into wine, tragedy into triumph. The promise is there. Accept it. Receive it. Rejoice!

God, help me to dance in the joy of your promises. Amen.

DECEMBER 7 — BE FAITHFUL

His master replied, "Well done, good and faithful servant! You have been faithful with a few things; I will put you in charge of many things. Come and share your master's happiness!"
—Matthew 25:21

In the working world, happiness comes from pleasing your earthly boss. In our Christian walk, happiness comes from faithfulness to our heavenly "boss." God gives each of us many opportunities to witness to our faith, and our happiness is tied to how well we handle these opportunities. Are we faithful to our convictions? Do we use the gifts and talents we have been given, or do we hide our abilities for fear of failure? Are we good stewards of the many things God has given us—family, friends, the earth—or are we more concerned with our own selfish interests? If we are faithful, God will reward our efforts and give us many gifts and graces for our service, including the happiness we all seek.

God, help me to be your faithful servant in all the things you ask of me. Amen.

DECEMBER 8 — PRAISE GOD THROUGH MUSIC

Then Israel sang this song: "Spring up, O well!"
—Numbers 21:17

We both like music and often use it as a means of worship and celebration. One of the songs we sing with our youth group is "Spring up, O Well." It is a song of happiness and joy, meant to be sung with great enthusiasm. Almost everywhere you find a passage about singing in the Bible, you find a song of happiness and celebration. God meant for us to be a happy people, and music is one way to express our happiness. Musical styles change over the years, and what you listen to is probably not what your parents listen to, even in worship music. Whatever the style and wherever you hear it, remember that music is a great means of expressing your love for God and celebrating all of the gifts we receive from our loving Lord.

God, thank you for happy music. May your song always be in my heart. Amen.

DECEMBER 9 — SING TO GOD— EVEN IF YOU CAN'T CARRY A TUNE!

May the righteous be glad and rejoice before God; may they be happy and joyful. Sing to God, sing praise to his name, extol him who rides on the clouds—his name is the LORD—and rejoice before him. —Psalm 68:3-4

I've been singing since I was a little girl. I've sung in choirs, chorales, and bands off and on for as long as I can remember. I've always found a special release in singing—release from tension, troubles, and the general blahs of life. When I sing songs of praise to God, I am blessed because I am doing something I love while sharing God's word with others. Music is one of God's best gifts—a gift to be shared with others and with God. It always makes me happy when I can sing to our God of great gifts.

Even if you think you can't sing, sing anyway! Your song will be beautiful to God's ears!

God, teach me to praise you in song, and help me to make music with my life. Amen.

DECEMBER 10 — LET YOUR HAPPINESS SHOW

A happy heart makes the face cheerful, but heartache crushes the spirit. —Proverbs 15:13

What you feel inside often shows on your face. When you are happy, it shows. Other people are the same way. How often do we notice how our friends look? Are they down? Are they upset? Sometimes we are so busy with our own lives that we don't notice the pain in those around us, yet this can be one of our best clues as we try to be God's witnesses in this world. We need to be aware of those we meet who are in need of encouragement, a hug, or just a kind word. Let your happiness show and broadcast the God who is within you, but also be looking for those who need a little extra care today.

God, let my happy heart show today and help me to encourage those around me. Amen.

FIND YOUR HOPE IN CHRIST

Praise be to the God and Father of our Lord Jesus Christ! In his great mercy he has given us new birth into a living hope through the resurrection of Jesus Christ from the dead. —1 Peter 1:3

Hope is a very precious thing. It is what makes it possible for us to keep going when all that's around us seems to be falling apart. It is what keeps us struggling when all reason says that "resistance is futile!" It is what gives us the strength to survive all the things that happen on this road of life. Where does this hope come from? From the risen Christ, God incarnate, who lives in us and through us and gives us life. On those dark days when you think you can't go any farther, just reach out to this Christ who promises us new life and hope eternal. You will not be disappointed.

God, thank you for giving me hope today. Amen.

DRAW STRENGTH FROM GOD

May our Lord Jesus Christ himself and God our Father, who loved us and by his grace gave us eternal encouragement and good hope, encourage your hearts and strengthen you in every good deed and word. —2 Thessalonians 2:16-17

Did you ever have one of "those" days? You know, when everything goes crazy and nothing seems to work right and your friends all seem distant and uncaring? The day starts bad and goes downhill from there, and you tend to get a little discouraged and cranky, and all the people around you seem cranky, too. Well, God is present in that day, too. God's Spirit is present in the tough times as well as the good times, providing hope and encouragement and strength. What an amazing God! If God can put up with us on "those" days, then God truly loves us like no other. I like that.

God, please be with me today, especially if it is one of "those" days. Amen.

BE THANKFUL

Let the peace of Christ rule in your hearts, since as members of one body you were called to peace. And be thankful.
—Colossians 3:15

thankfulness

when i am cold
and the fire is bold
i am thankful

when the game is on live
and i'm home by five
i am thankful

when the chili is spicy
and the water is icy
i am thankful

when the news is all good
and it's quiet in the hood
i am thankful

when the burgers are hot
and the root beer is not
i am thankful

when the story is done
and no one has run
i am thankful

when navajo and creek
sit side by side and eat
i am thankful

when black, brown or white
is not a reason to fight
i am thankful

when God is at hand
and there's peace in the land
i am thankful

God, thank you, thank you, thank you! Amen.

TALK TO GOD WHEN YOU'RE FEELING DOWN

Even youths will faint and be weary, and the young will fall exhausted; but those who wait for the LORD shall renew their strength, they shall mount up with wings like eagles, they shall run and not be weary, they shall walk and not faint.
—Isaiah 40:30-31 (NRSV)

Do you ever get down—*really* down? It's a condition that seems to come with being human. Things start piling up on you, and you get stressed and depressed and confused and cranky. I'm not sure you can keep that from happening from time to time, but I am sure of how you can get out of it when it does happen: Talk to God! God promises to renew us and stand beside us and help us—not only to survive, but also to thrive and to soar above it all. That's what I call a real cure!

God, help me to soar today, no matter what happens. Amen.

SEEK GOD WITH ALL YOUR HEART

"For I know the plans I have for you," declares the LORD, "plans to prosper you and not to harm you, plans to give you hope and a future. Then you will call upon me and come and pray to me, and I will listen to you. You will seek me and find me when you seek me with all your heart."
—Jeremiah 29:11-13 (NIV)

God has plans for us—big plans! How about that? And we thought we were just drifting along, kinda going nowhere. God has plans, and all we have to do is follow. That's easier than getting lost, even though we don't always like to ask directions (especially us guys). God has plans to give us hope—what a great gift! And a future, too. Sounds like we better latch onto this plan—keep in touch with this God. "Seek me with all your heart" sounds reasonable and uncomplicated. A God who listens to us when we pray and gives hope and a future—guess we'd better sign on for this!

God, thank you for this wonderful offer of hope and a future. Amen.

DECEMBER 16
SPEND TIME ALONE WITH GOD

I say to myself, "The LORD is my portion; therefore I will wait for him." The LORD is good to those whose hope is in him, to the one who seeks him; it is good to wait quietly for the salvation of the LORD.
—Lamentations 3:24-26

Our youth group can be noisy and energetic, and the energy is contagious. We like to see them actively enjoying whatever activity we may be doing. We also encourage them to try TAG: Time Alone with God. In a world filled with noise of every kind, it can be hard to listen for God; and in a world moving at the speed of sound bytes, it can be hard to wait. Yet God wants us to listen and to wait. Listen, for God will speak to you. Wait, for God will come to you. In these things, there is great hope.

God, help me to listen and to wait for you. Amen.

DECEMBER 17
PUT YOUR HOPE ONLY IN GOD

Show me your ways, O LORD, teach me your paths; guide me in your truth and teach me, for you are God my Savior, and my hope is in you all day long.
—Psalm 25:4-5

When I was a small boy, my hopes were pretty limited. I hoped for the things I could see and understand, like a peanut butter sandwich or a new puppy. My world did not go far beyond the family farm, nor did my dreams. As I grew older, I began to discover the world outside, and I wasn't pleased with what I found. I expected it to be like home. It wasn't. The older I got, the more I realized that the only constant in my life is God, and that I can set my hope in him without fear of failure or rejection. Since that realization, I have not feared the world or anything in it. I have found peace in the teachings of my God, and safety in his care. Freedom. Hope. Safety. What more could a child of God ask for?

Dear Lord, thank you for the hope, freedom, and safety that come from following you. Amen.

READ THE BIBLE

For everything that was written in the past was written to teach us, so that through endurance and the encouragement of the Scriptures we might have hope. —Romans 15:4

Why should we read the Bible? It's just an old book, right? Clearly, the Bible is more than an "old book"; it is a very important tool in our daily lives. Our faith is based on the Scriptures, the Word of God. It is from these texts that we draw our hope and our faith and our solace. In them, we learn of God's love for us from the beginning of time, and of the patience and forgiveness needed on God's part to maintain the relationship. We all need to read and hear the good words of the Scriptures on a daily basis to help us maintain our hope and our faith. They are God's words, spoken to us, for life.

Thank you, God, for revealing yourself to us through the Bible. Amen.

PUT ON THE ARMOR OF GOD

But since we belong to the day, let us be self-controlled, putting on faith and love as a breastplate, and the hope of salvation as a helmet. —1 Thessalonians 5:8

Bicycle helmets, football helmets, chest protectors, chin guards—we manage to protect almost every part of our bodies today. Why not our spirits as well? Just as the protective gear used in sports keeps us from physical harm, so also the armor of God can protect our spirits and our souls as we play the game of life. The trick is to put on the protective armor without putting on a mask as well. We need to be in control of our lives without being controlling of others or being phony. Don't hide the real you behind a mask, but do be sure to put on the protective armor of God's love and eternal hope.

God, help me to wear my helmet of salvation today without wearing a mask. Amen.

DECEMBER 20
REMEMBER THAT YOU HAVE THE HOPE OF ETERNAL LIFE

So that, having been justified by [Jesus'] grace, we might become heirs having the hope of eternal life. —Titus 3:7

Grace: God's Riches At Christ's Expense. We have the riches of God at our fingertips because Jesus made the sacrifice for us. We have hope; and when we have hope, anything is possible. No matter how far down we think we've fallen, we have hope. No matter how dark the future looks, we have hope. No matter what our friends say, we have hope. Jesus died to save us, and he lives to make us free from despair. We are heirs of God. God has promised us that we will inherit life eternal, and that, above all, is reason to hope.

God, help me to remember that your grace is always there and that I have a reason to hope. Amen.

DECEMBER 21
WALK WITH JESUS

Though you have not seen him, you love him; and even though you do not see him now, you believe in him and are filled with an inexpressible and glorious joy. —1 Peter 1:8

It may seem difficult to believe in this Jesus from 2,000 years ago—until you realize that he is just as real today as when he walked upon the Sea of Galilee. This is the real key to our faith, the great reality that separates us from other religions: Our God is alive! Our Jesus walks with us hand in hand. With this sure knowledge, we can go through the daily struggles with a calm that is not of this world, a calm that comes from our awesome God. This is certainly reason for joy and celebration. We know that Jesus is with us, and we feel his presence continually, sometimes with an intensity that is beyond words. When this happens, be silent and listen.

Jesus, thank you for being with me today. Amen.

DECEMBER 22 — SHARE YOUR FAITH

I have no greater joy than to hear that my children are walking in the truth.
—3 John 1:4

You might be surprised to know that your youth leaders and other adults in the church worry about you and really care about your faith journey and your relationship with God. We have often been concerned about some of the youth we minister to. Sometimes we don't know if they understand or are even listening. But God is faithful, and the Word always rings true. Great joy comes from seeing God working in the lives of those you minister to. Need some real joy in your life? Try sharing your faith with those around you, and then watch what God can do.

Please, God, let me experience the joy of seeing your hand at work in the lives of others. Amen.

DECEMBER 23 — FIND JOY IN THE UNEXPECTED

So I commend the enjoyment of life, because nothing is better for [people] under the sun than to eat and drink and be glad. Then joy will accompany [them] in [their] work all the days of the life God has given [them] under the sun.
—Ecclesiastes 8:15

We had an unusual experience one weekend. We were on a short trip to deliver some computer equipment to one of the church camps on the other side of the state. A simple and pleasant trip, we thought. About two hours into the trip, our car quit and had to be towed in for repairs. After leaving the garage, we decided to drop the equipment at a closer camp, only ten miles away, and then return home. The car quit again before we reached the camp! With help from some loving friends and kind strangers, we found someone to fix the car and were able to stay at the camp for the night. Where's the joy in this? In all these troubles, we saw the hand of God in the hands that helped us; and we saw the face of God in the beauty of the camp in early spring.

Life doesn't always go as planned, but there is joy to be found in every day if we look for it.

God, help me to find joy in the unexpected. Amen.

DECEMBER 24 KEEP YOUR FOCUS ON JESUS

Therefore, since we are surrounded by such a great cloud of witnesses, let us throw off everything that hinders and the sin that so easily entangles, and let us run with perseverance the race marked out for us. Let us fix our eyes on Jesus, the author and perfecter of our faith, who for the joy set before him endured the cross, scorning its shame, and sat down at the right hand of the throne of God.
—Hebrews 12:1-2

Living the Christian life is often like running an obstacle course. There are so many things that get in our way as we try to follow Christ—friends, school activities, world events, and even church. We are easily distracted by what we see and hear around us, by the world going by, and by our own failures. Sometimes it's hard to find the joy that is supposed to be ours as Christians.

It's reassuring to know that Christ was aware of the distractions and that by watching his example, we can see a way out of our unhappiness. Christ was constantly aware of the goal, the target, the plan. He kept his eyes on the finish line and turned the struggles of getting there into joyful acts of praise and service. Our challenge is to maintain that focus and to remain aware of the many people who are supporting us and praying for us. We have the opportunity to just go for it!

Dear God, please help me to keep my eyes on you and to discover the joy that comes from serving you. Amen.

DECEMBER 25 CELEBRATE JESUS!

The desert and the parched land will be glad; the wilderness will rejoice and blossom. Like the crocus, it will burst into bloom; it will rejoice greatly and shout for joy.
—Isaiah 35:1-2

The world was waiting—waiting for the Messiah. They had been waiting for years—centuries, actually. Waiting with the same anticipation that you feel as you wait for your sixteenth birthday or graduation day. Then it happened. Jesus the Christ was born, and all of heaven and earth rejoiced. Peace and good will were in the air; beauty burst into bloom on the face of the planet. For a while, everything was new and exciting. However, just as your excitement fades after your birthday or any big event, so also the world's excitement and joy for Jesus faded; and they turned from him. The beauty was still there; the reason for rejoicing still existed. But other things got in the way. As we celebrate again the coming of the Messiah, keep the excitement, see the beauty, and feel the joy of knowing the King of Heaven is with you always.

Happy Birthday, Jesus. Help me remember that you are worth waiting for. Amen.

"GET LOUD" ABOUT YOUR GOD

Shout aloud and sing for joy, people of Zion, for great is the Holy One of Israel among you. —Isaiah 12:6

We are the people of Zion, the followers of the God of Israel. From ancient times we have worshipped this God with joyful songs and praises. Today we can cheer for our favorite sports team and our favorite movie or TV star, but we're kind of hesitant when it comes to getting loud about our God. Why is that? Is this not the same God? Are we not still God's children?

Be joyful in your worship and energetic in your praise. Let the world know that this God is the one true God who is worthy of all glory and praise. Be joyful in your service, for there is no shame in being associated with this God and no greater glory than feeling the presence of this God in your life.

God of ancient times, thank you for being God of the present, too. Amen.

CELEBRATE AND SHARE THE GIFTS OF CHRIST

The angel said to them, "Do not be afraid. I bring you good news of great joy that will be for all the people. Today in the town of David a Savior has been born to you; he is Christ the Lord." —Luke 2:10-11

The most joyful news ever received by the people of this world: a Savior has been born—hope has been born! In a world that is often short on both joy and hope, it is good to remind ourselves that Christ came to bring us joy and hope and life eternal. It is the reason we celebrate Christ's birth with such enthusiasm; we *all* were given the gifts of hope, joy, and life. The gifts we give to one another are our way of sharing God's gifts to us— reminding one another of the goodness of our Savior. Joy to the world!

Thank you, God, for sending a Savior into this world. Amen.

DECEMBER 28

REJOICE IN YOUR SALVATION

With joy you will draw water from the wells of salvation. In that day you will say: "Give thanks to the LORD, call on his name; make known among the nations what he has done, and proclaim that his name is exalted. Sing to the LORD, for he has done glorious things; let this be known to all the world. " —Isaiah 12:3-5

What a word picture this scripture evokes! As a young man, I lived in rural areas where wells were an important part of our lives. I recall reading this verse and seeing the picture in my mind—drawing salvation out of the well like a thirsty kid on a hot summer day draws water from the water well. Water is the symbol of baptism, of belonging, and of new life. What a joy it is for us to be able to go to that well of salvation and renew our relationship with God, remember our baptism, recognize our kinship, and drink in the new life waiting for us. When that happens, we can't help but share that joy with those around us.

Thank you, God, for never letting the well of salvation go dry. Amen.

DECEMBER 29

LET GOD BE YOUR SHIELD

The LORD is my strength and my shield; my heart trusts in him, and I am helped. My heart leaps for joy and I will give thanks to him in song. —Psalm 28:7

Now there's a pleasant thought to start the day: God is our body armor! No matter what the world throws at us, God is there; and we have a reason to be joyful. While we live in this world and have to deal with the problems it presents, our joy is in the Lord, who protects us. We're not out there flying solo as we try to live our lives in God's image, because that same God is our strength and our security. Nothing can harm our soul, our spirit, as long as we maintain that shield of faith, that body armor of prayer.

Hey, God, thanks for shielding me with your love today. Amen.

GIVE YOUR FEARS TO GOD

The LORD is my light and my salvation—whom shall I fear? The LORD is the stronghold of my life—of whom shall I be afraid?
—Psalm 27:1

No fear? Yeah, right! Who do they think they're kidding? We have been afraid many times in our ministry to youth. Afraid that we aren't up to the task. Afraid that the youth won't understand what we're trying to say. Afraid that some of the youth won't make it to adulthood. Then, the reassurance comes—"The Lord is my light and my salvation"—and we're back into the swing of things. Many things can make us fearful in our lives, but only our God can conquer all those fears and give us the joy of living we were meant to have—in God's care.

God, help me remember your strength when I am fearful. Amen.

FOLLOW WHERE GOD LEADS

The precepts of the LORD are right, giving joy to the heart. The commands of the LORD are radiant, giving light to the eyes.
—Psalm 19:8

Do you ever wonder where God is leading you? We wondered when God first lead us into youth ministry. Following the call was challenging, but God had a plan; and God gave our eyes the light to see it and our hearts the courage to believe it. When God calls you, and he surely will, try not to be blind to the possibilities. Follow where God leads, and your life will be joyful as the way is opened before you. God lights the way and enlightens the soul for those who have the courage to follow.

Help me, O God, to be courageous when you call me. Amen.